ECHOES FROM THE WEST

Verda Spickelmier

Verda Spickelmier

ECHOES FROM THE WEST

iUniverse, Inc.
Bloomington

Echoes from the West

iUniverse books may be ordered through booksellers or by contacting:
iUniverse
1663 Liberty Drive
Bloomington, IN 47403
www.iuniverse.com

1-800-Authors (1-800-288-4677)

ISBN: 978-1-4620-4080-3 (sc)
ISBN: 978-1-4620-4081-0 (e)
ISBN: 978-1-4620-4082-7 (dj)

Printed in the United States of America

iUniverse rev. date: 8/26/2011

CHAPTER 1
1828

WASHINGTON, DC

President John Quincy Adams rose early. The night had given him fitful sleep. A glance out the window of the newly rebuilt Executive Mansion revealed wintry skies. He slapped his burgeoning thighs and grumbled, "Will this weather never break? A fast swim in the Potomac is what I need!"

On honest reflection, he knew the weather was not the cause of his lack of exercise and his increasing weight. He conducted a mental run-through of his upcoming day. It was typical of all his days since he had been elected president by the House on February 9, 1825. It took all his time and energy to meet the steady procession of congressmen and department heads who demanded his attention. Thrown in were a few diplomatic parties. Fortunately, Mrs. Adams relieved him of planning for those. Her entertainment of the Marquis de Lafayette of France had been brilliant.

Today, he thought, *I must talk first to Clay. I hope the buzzards in Congress aren't on Henry again with that corrupt-bargain nonsense. He was the most competent man I could have appointed as secretary of state, regardless of whether he threw his influence behind me in the election.*

Another trouble area came to mind. He must meet again with

1

Andrew Jackson and his supporters on the tariff bill. Not only did the tariff battle between New England and the South rage on, but now there was also pressure being exerted to throw open the West's public-domain land for expansion. And there was that enormous wilderness area called the Oregon Country, which sprawled west of the Rockies to the Pacific Ocean and north of Spanish California to the southern line of Russian-claimed territory. Before becoming president, he had, as secretary of state, negotiated Spain and Russia out of the Oregon territory and by treaty established a peaceful coexistence with Britain. But that had been nearly ten years ago, and the treaty was due to expire—or, with luck, be extended.

"God help us," Adams entreated as he descended the stairs. "Oregon Country! Would we be better off without it?"

STEENS MOUNTAIN, OREGON COUNTRY

Midway up the west side of the mountain, in a U-shaped valley, stood the winter shelters of a small Wada Tika band of Northern Paiutes. The valley, one of many formed on the mountain by ancient glaciers, had an aspen grove at its entrance. Farther on, a few willow trees grew beside a stream. Pine trees grew among the rocks on the valley walls and gave some protection from the wind and snow to the shelters on the valley floor.

Each shelter, built around a fire pit, was constructed of a dozen or so willow-tree poles pulled together in a cone shape and covered by bulrush mats. Two holes were left: one at the top for smoke to escape, and the other near the ground as an entryway to the east.

It was early morning, and a young boy crept from one of the shelters. He scanned the sky. He was ready for spring. The fragile nature of the basin land did not support permanent settlements. During the mild seasons of the year, family groups and small bands met and lived together, but before winter came, they separated and prepared winter shelters separated by varying distances.

When spring arrived, flocks of geese, ducks, pelicans, and small birds returned by the thousands. All birds were welcome signs of spring, but the geese, flying rapidly high overhead in great V-shaped formations, were the most welcome. Their return was the signal for the bands wintering on the mountain to meet at the lake.

As the boy scanned the sky, he heard, far off in the distance, the unmistakable, honking cry he had been waiting to hear.

"Nagita!" he shouted. "Nagita!"

He knew it would not take the group long to break camp and start down the mountain. No one had died at camp during the winter, so no shelters needed to be burned. All the shelters would be left for the next group that decided to winter there.

His mother would gather up the baskets she and his sister had woven from slender willow wands during the winter; some baskets had been woven loosely for gathering, and others had been woven watertight. He would carry the braided rope of fire.

He could now see the wavering V-shaped formation, and as others emerged from the shelters, he pointed and shouted again, "Nagita!"

When the band began their downward move, a wintry chill remained in the air. Both men and women wore their rabbit-skin blankets belted about them. Only the men wore moccasins made from hides; the women and children wore rush-woven sandals. Antelopes were occasionally captured in the basin, but rabbits were as important to the Wada Tika as buffalo were to the Plains Indians.

The area, called a basin because the waters of its streams and lakes remained within it, was dotted with sinks, or low areas that held runoff water from the melting snow. The streams would either dry up or empty into one of the basin's lakes, which increased and decreased in size, depending on the amount of water evaporation.

The Wada Tika, like other Paiutes, were not warriors, and their harsh environment protected them from aggressive cultures. Honor lay in the ability to survive, but, although resources were a premium, they were taught as children to be generous and never deny food to those in need. Only what was needed was taken from nature, and something was given back in return. Daily prayers were made to the Great Spirit. The dead were mourned, even though the living knew that those who had died watched over them.

Late in the afternoon, the band reached the bank of a small, shallow runoff stream, where they decided to spend the night. The young girls gathered wood for a fire to heat rocks that would be dropped into water held in one of the tightly woven willow baskets. The rocks would boil the water for a meal of pine-nut soup.

While the girls gathered wood, the women covered the distance from one bush to another with brush, creating shelters just high enough to crawl under for the night. After the meal of soup had been eaten, everyone was ready for a night's rest and anxious for morning, when they would continue the journey down the mountain.

They reached the lake on the third day, while the sun was still high in the sky. The women, impatient for fresh, green food, dropped their rabbit skins on the ground, waded into the marsh, and pulled up the new cattail shoots. Skillfully peeling off the soggy brown leaves with their thumbnails, they filled their baskets with the white spears. That evening, everyone ate their fill of tender cattail shoots and ground squirrel meat roasted in the coals.

After their meal, they gathered in a circle for story time. The storyteller told the story of the beginning of the world.

"In the beginning of the world," he began, "there were only two: our father and mother. We are all their children.

"At first, in the beginning, they had four children: two girls and two boys. One girl and one boy had dark skin. The other girl and boy had light skin. They were a happy family. The sun warmed the family. The rain gave them water. There was food for everyone. They had nothing to do but play and be happy."

The storyteller's voice grew sad. "But after a while, they became cross with one another. They began to fight with each other. Our father and mother were aggrieved. What could they do to be a happy family again?"

The storyteller sighed. "Nothing. Nothing they did stopped the fighting. So our father separated the children by a word. He said, 'Depart from each other, you cruel children—go far away and do not seek each other's lives.'

"So the light girl and boy disappeared, and our father and mother saw them no more. They grieved, but they knew their light children were happy. By and by, the dark children grew into many families. The light children grew into many families, too. Someday, they will send someone to meet us and heal all the old trouble. Then we will all be a happy family again."

The moon was rising over the lake as the people walked to their shelters after the storytelling.

The young boy lay awake, listening to the soft sighing of the wind and the night singing of the marsh wren. As his eyes closed, a moorhen broke the nighttime calm with its wild, excited call. Like hysterical laughter, it spread through the marsh and into the shelters on shore.

Many groups gathered at the lake during the days that followed. The women scratched and dug for roots to be boiled and eaten. They gathered the first leaves of the squaw cabbage, which had to be boiled twice to remove the bitterness. The men made boatlike rafts of dried tule tied in bundles. Searching for water-fowl eggs, the men paddled the rafts in and out of the clumps of reeds that grew close to the water's edge.

The men were netting ducks one afternoon and the women had just returned from gathering mustard seed when a group of people arrived from the Trout Eaters tribe in the south. They brought a strange, strange story.

The story was so strange that a special meeting was called. The men sat in an inner circle; the women sat in a circle around the men; the children tumbled about in a third circle.

The storyteller began by telling of a dream had by the oldest grandfather in their tribe. The grandfather dreamed that early one morning, two women were fanning chaff from seed. They were busy at their work, in an open space, when they heard strange voices.

Frightened, they looked up and saw two men with hair on their faces walking toward them, leading two strange creatures with ears like jackrabbits and big eyes.

The women screamed, threw down their baskets, and ran. In his dream, the grandfather was not afraid, so he went to meet the two strange men. They did not seem to understand him when he talked to them, and he did not understand what they said, so the two men turned and walked away.

"What really happened," the storyteller from the southern tribe said, "was almost like the dream. Not two, but one woman was fanning chaff from seed when she heard voices. She looked up to see two men with hair on their faces, leading two big animals that had ears like jackrabbits, long faces, and very big eyes. Like in the dream, the woman screamed, threw down her basket, and ran back to camp.

"The grandfather, hearing her scream, rushed out but only in time to see the rear ends of the two animals that to him looked more like the hind parts of deer than jackrabbits. The way they walked, however, was not like deer or antelope or even mountain sheep, and they were a peculiar brown in color.

"A few days later, a hunting party met these two men with their animals. The men and the animals looked so strange and ugly, they frightened the hunters. The hunters stoned them all to death."

TAOS, NEW MEXICO

Ewing Young, thirty-two years old and six feet, two inches tall, leaned against the adobe wall of his dwelling in Taos, New Mexico. With brooding eyes, he studied the gathering clouds. It was too warm for snow. Rain, maybe. His taut body straightened instinctively at the sound of approaching footsteps.

Young relaxed and almost smiled as a thin, short young man appeared from around the corner of the building.

"Mornin', Kit." He nodded.

Sandy-haired Christopher "Kit" Carson had something more than the morning on his mind. He coughed nervously before he said, "Mr. Young, I appreciate you taking me in last fall. I know you had lots on your mind, what with the governor taking away your furs …"

Young stopped him with a raised hand. "I needed a cook. You came looking for a job." To Young, it had been as simple as that—no questions asked.

Carson shifted uneasily. Without wasting more time, he said, "I want to go back to the States."

Young's gaze returned to the clouds. "Travelin' by yourself?"

"Yes, sir," Carson answered. "Got a good horse. Good gun. Should be other parties on the trail."

Young lowered his gaze to Carson's eager blue eyes and extended his hand. "Ever come back and want to learn the trappin' business, look me up. I'll be goin' out again soon as Henry Clay gets a passport to me."

Carson gripped Young's hand before he disappeared again around the building.

Ewing Young, by trade a carpenter, was a trapper and a fighter. He had trapped in Tennessee as a boy and in Missouri as a young man. His grandfather had fought in the American Revolution; his father and uncle had fought the Cherokees and the Creeks. Young fought whatever needed fighting.

Living in Taos wasn't planned; it happened. He had bought a farm in Missouri the first month of 1822 and in the spring had gotten word that his friend William Becknell was forming another wagon train heading for Santa Fe. The year before, Becknell had made a fortune taking a caravan of trading goods to Santa Fe, the capital of Spain's province of New Mexico. He had traded his buttons, razors, cooking utensils, and brightly colored cottons and silks for Mexican gold and silver.

Young was more interested in adventure than farming, so he sold his farm and bought in as a third partner of Becknell's second undertaking. Santa Fe, Becknell told him, was seething with excitement over impending Mexican independence from Spain.

Three hundred years earlier, Spanish adventurer Hernando Cortés, with a six-hundred-man army of his own and reinforcements from local Indian groups, conquered the powerful Aztec Nation. King Charles I of Spain rewarded the conquerors with huge estates and in 1522 named Cortes governor and captain-general of the country, now called New Spain.

The area of New Spain was extended in 1540 when Francisco Coronado led a force of three hundred Spaniards and several hundred Indians farther into the Southwest and claimed those lands for Spain.

The high posts in the government and also in the Roman Catholic Church were given to people born in Spain. As the years passed, people of pure Spanish ancestry born in New Spain came to be called Creoles. Those of mixed Spanish and Indian ancestry were called Mestizos. People of pure Indian ancestry continued to live much as they had before the Spanish came.

By 1800, the Creoles wanted independence from Spain. Late on the night of September 15, 1810, Miguel Hidalgo y Costilla, a Creole priest, launched the Mexican War of Independence. Various struggles and leaders followed. Governors changed hands rapidly and waxed hot and cold over trade with Americans.

The current governor wanted gun powder, and that was what Becknell and Young loaded in their supply wagons. By early summer, however, when the wagon train reached New Mexico, they found Mexico had already won its independence from Spain.

Young dissolved his partnership with Becknell and stayed on in New Mexico, intending to practice his trade as a carpenter. He soon discovered a more lucrative occupation and became a leader in the fur trade of the Southwest. Furs, of no demand in the warm Mexican climate, brought a good price in Europe. The easiest fur to trap and ship was beaver, and beaver hats in Europe were at a premium.

The Mexican territory to the north and west of Santa Fe was unsettled by Europeans. The wild, rocky terrain harbored an abundance of small creeks and streams. Beaver colonies worked every creek and every stream. In the fall and winter, when the fur of the beaver was at its prime, the trappers worked the beaver colonies. When spring broke, the trappers loaded their winter catch and headed for civilization.

Young moved to Taos, a town situated on the southern edge of the pine-covered high country and looking north into the Rockies. There he set up his headquarters and recruited trappers. At first he supervised his men by trapping along with them.

By the winter of 1826–1827, an abundance of trappers had saturated the area, and Young, forced to stay in Taos for health reasons, sent his men out in groups of two or three with instructions to follow their established routes and work the streams as usual. In the spring, two trappers failed to return. Another group had met up with the two early in the season. They reported the two were disgruntled with the increased number of trappers and complained the streams were overtrapped. They were heading out of the territory, they said, going farther north.

Besides losing track of two of his men, Young also lost his furs. Between the beginning and the end of the trapping season, a change of governorship was made. The new governor, attempting to curb the activities of the Americans in his province, seized whatever furs he could get, and Young was one who had his furs taken away.

Young, although he had lost his furs for the season, was determined to continue trapping. He sent off a request to Secretary of State Henry Clay asking for an official passport. When it came, he planned to set off for the Mexican area called California.

Young stood a long while by the adobe wall, thinking of the trapping season he had been forced to spend in Taos instead of in the field. He knew he had needed the rest. A Mexican doctor had confirmed Young's need for peace and quiet to cure an illness characterized by fever and constipation. And during the winter in Taos, he had met and fallen in love with the beautiful, dark-eyed Maria Josefa Tafoya. His only regret today was not knowing what had become of his two trappers who had gone north. He wondered if they were alive or dead.

The faint rustling sound of a skirt brought him back to the present.

"Maria?" he said softly.

OREGON COUNTRY

Jedediah Smith, American trapper, relaxed against a log and gazed into the campfire. It had been another long day of driving three hundred horses and mules packed with furs across rough terrain. Two of his nineteen men were posted as guards. The rest were asleep. Smith had been ordered out of California by Mexican officials and was now in Oregon territory, heading for the British Fort Vancouver where he hoped to sell his furs to John McLoughlin.

Smith understood the beaver-fur business. It was run for profit. Success depended on finding the most economical way to transform raw animal pelts from wilderness streams to hats worn on heads of genteel Eastern and European gentlemen. After a winter spent trailing and communicating with British trapper Peter Ogden, he understood the business even better. The British, early on, built forts on navigable waterways where Indians delivered their furs for barter. The furs were then transported down the rivers for marketing. Later, the British employed their own trappers, who were sent out in parties supervised by a handpicked leader. Their focus, of course, was still on furs, and they made no discernment as to the bearer of the furs for sale, whether they were British, French, Russian, Indian, or American. Thus, Smith expected McLoughlin would pay him top price for his furs.

Smith rose, stretched, and walked toward his saddle. It was a warm evening—no need for a campfire except heat for cooking and light to read by. Taking a large black Bible from his saddlebag, he sat down again and turned to the chapter of Isaiah. After reading awhile, he closed his Bible and thought about the man who had given it to him. Dr. Simons had taught him to read and write and also given him a copy of the Lewis and Clark journals, a book almost as dear to Smith as his Bible. From Dr. Simons and the journals, he had learned how President Thomas Jefferson in early 1803 had proposed to Congress that a Corps of Discovery be organized to cross the land between the Mississippi River and the Pacific Ocean. Jefferson had based his Corps of Discovery proposal on the fact that Capt. Robert Gray, an American, had discovered the Columbia River, a great river in the West that emptied into the Pacific Ocean.

In 1787 Gray had been hired by Boston merchants to take a cargo of buttons, beads, blue cloth, and bits of iron and copper on his ship, the Columbia, from Boston, around South America's Cape Horn to the Pacific coast. The cargo was used to barter with Natives on the coast for pelts of sea otters. Gray then sailed on to the Orient and bartered the pelts for tea, silk, and spices, which he returned to the Boston merchants who sold them in the United States for a good profit.

Five years later, Gray was again sailing along the Pacific coast. At latitudes 46o 53', he came across a great flow of muddy water fanning from the shore. He believed the muddy waters must be coming from the mouth of a great river—the Great River of the West! Entering the river's mouth would be treacherous. The turbulent waters, he knew, could smash his ship unless he entered at the right time. He waited and watched. At eight o'clock one morning there came a convergence of currents, tide, and wind. Gray gave the command, and his ship crashed through the breakers and sailed safely into the river waters. Gray, proud of his ship, gave her name to the river: the Columbia River.

Because of Gray's discovery, the United States claimed a vested interest in the Oregon Country. When Jefferson became president, the western boundary of the United States was the Mississippi River. The land between the Mississippi River and the Oregon Country was called the Louisiana Territory and claimed by France, who had only recently acquired it from Spain. Jefferson's plan was for the Corps of Discovery to pass through the French-claimed lands and explore the Oregon Country. Congress approved his proposal.

Jefferson promptly appointed his personal secretary, twenty-eight-year-old Meriwether Lewis, accomplished frontiersman, to lead the expedition. Lewis appointed his friend, thirty-two-year-old Army Lieutenant William Clark, as second in command.

While Lewis and Clark were recruiting robust, healthy, hardy young men for the Corps, French Emperor Napoleon Bonaparte, in desperate need of funding for his European military ventures, sold the Louisiana Territory to the US government for $15 million.

Jefferson was then free to assign the Corps the additional task of obtaining all the information they could about the Native peoples and natural features of the newly-acquired land.

It took more than two years, but the Corps made the trip successfully. On their way back, on August 12, 1806, traveling on the Missouri River, they met two American trappers from Illinois coming upriver in a canoe. One of Lewis and Clark's men, John

Colter, asked permission to accompany the two back into the wilds. Permission was granted.

While all this was happening, Jedediah Smith was growing up with his family in the Susquehanna Valley of southern New York State; and later in Erie County, Pennsylvania; and then in Ashland County, Ohio. There, on his twenty-first birthday, his father blessed him with God's protection and gave him leave to go where he would. Smith left his family, traveled through Illinois, and followed the Mississippi River to Saint Louis.

In Saint Louis, he walked, awestruck, through the town, watching and listening. Many stories circulated of the mountains and the west. News of the Corps' successful trip had spread rapidly, and trapping companies immediately began organizing in Saint Louis. The first group to depart, he learned, was headed by Manuel Lisa, a man of Spanish descent born in New Orleans. With backing from several Illinois merchants, Lisa had organized a crew of forty men. They had scarcely departed on April 19, 1807, when they met John Colter paddling back alone downriver. Lisa picked him up and hired him as a guide.

Following the British technique, at the junction of the Bighorn and Yellowstone Rivers, Lisa built a fort of logs, which he christened Fort Raymond after his infant son. Here he set up his trading stock of trinkets, liquor, knives, blankets, and rifles and sent his men out to persuade Indians to bring in furs.

Colter set out on snowshoes, carrying only a rifle and minimal supplies on his back. By spring he had recruited five hundred Crow and Flathead Indians who were willing to accompany him to Fort Raymond with their pelts.

As Smith had found in his own bitter experience, some Indians were friendly, and some were not. One tribe that no one had yet been successful in winning over was the Blackfeet. On the way back to Fort Raymond, Colter and his group met a band of Blackfeet warriors. The peaceful, unarmed Indians accompanying Colter scattered. Colter, shot in the leg, scarcely made it back to Fort Raymond.

Other trappers were more successful in bringing in Indians and furs, and Lisa returned to Saint Louis with an impressive load of beaver pelts. The next season, he had no problem finding backers and soon formed the Missouri Fur Company. Among the directors were William Clark and Meriwether Lewis's brother Reuben. Lisa selected Andrew Henry to lead the first Missouri Fur Company flotilla, consisting of more than three hundred men.

Colter met them at the Great Bend of the Missouri River and marched them overland to Fort Raymond. Still trying to make friends with the Blackfeet, they went on to Three Forks in the heart of their country and built a small stockade.

Besides being Blackfeet country, this area turned out to also be grizzly-bear territory, and the grizzlies were no friendlier than the Blackfeet. After several trappers had been killed, Colter placed Andrew Henry in charge of the fort and left for Saint Louis to let the Missouri Fur Company directors know what was happening. This time he made it all the way to Saint Louis and decided not to go back to the wilds. He married and took up farming in Missouri.

When fall came and Colter had not returned, Andrew Henry abandoned the fort, and he and his men crossed the Continental Divide and built a trading post on the Snake River. He had underestimated the Blackfeet; they were unrelenting. When spring came, Henry closed the fort, made his way back to Saint Louis, and became a lead miner.

"And his move back," Smith reminisced, "is why I'm here."

Henry's neighbor in Saint Louis was William Ashley, who had moved to Saint Louis from Virginia. When Smith came to Saint Louis, Henry and Ashley had just formed a partnership and run an ad in the Missouri *Gazette*.

Smith remembered well the ad. "TO ENTERPRISING YOUNG MEN," it began. "The subscriber wishes to engage one hundred men, to ascend the river Missouri to its source, there to be employed for one, two or three years. For particulars, inquire of Major Andrew Henry, near the Lead Mines, in the County of Washington (who will ascend with, and command the party) or to the subscriber at Saint Louis. WM. H. ASHLEY."

Smith had faced Ashley's door with trepidation, but was promptly hired. On May 8, 1822, he was aboard a keelboat going up the Missouri.

Smith stretched once more and made ready for sleep. In his six years in the wilderness, he had been attacked by unfriendly Indians; seen both white men and Indians killed; seen men and horses collapse from fatigue and thirst in the desert; seen them freeze to death in the snow; and been mauled and disfigured by a grizzly bear. But he had also wintered with friendly Indians, and he had survived subzero nights, howling snowstorms, and gale-force desert winds. He had traveled with a Hudson Bay Company trapping party, seen the Great Salt Lake, crossed the Mojave Desert, and been welcomed at Mission San Gabriel in Spanish California one winter and accused of being a spy for the American government the next. He had found a pass through the mountains, and he had seen the ocean, the rivers, the plains of the West. Through it all, he had kept his faith in God.

If God chose to take me tonight, he thought, *I am ready and would die content and happy.*

FORT VANCOUVER, OREGON COUNTRY

Late at night, John McLoughlin was aroused by activity at the gates of the fort. A man stumbled in, barely alive, saying his name was Black, that he was a trapper with American Jedediah Smith, and that the rest of his party had been killed by Indians. The next morning, however, Jedediah Smith, John Turner, and one other trapper showed up.

Smith reported that ten days earlier, he and the two men with him had left the main camp by canoe, going upriver in search of the best route north. When they returned in the evening, they found only dead bodies in camp and had made their way to Fort Vancouver as quickly as they were able.

McLoughlin made the men comfortable and ordered a brigade headed by Tom McKay to return to the scene, bury the bodies, and retrieve what they could. He advised Smith and his men to remain at the fort until spring.

HUMBOLDT LAKE

Cousins to the northwest had come to the Trout Eaters' camp with a story of an event that had happened in their country.

The story began with a party of white men with many, many horses being spotted coming up from the south. They were traveling as close as they could to the shore of the ocean.

"Scouts watched the white men as they traveled," the cousin said. "Before long they wandered into the sand hills and were about to perish. The scouts went to their head man and told him what was happening.

"The head man called three hundred of his finest men. They went bravely into the sands and rescued the white men and all their horses. They found a safe camp for the white men and treated them to much food while they rested."

The storyteller continued, recounting how one of the white men left the camp and killed an elk. He brought it back to camp and hung it on a pole. A man from a different tribe came into camp. He saw the elk hanging on the pole and wondered if the meat was good. To check, he struck the elk with his knife.

"The white man's cook rushed over with a very large knife and struck the man who had struck the elk. He struck him so hard he cut off his ear. In the man's tribe, only runaway slaves and unfaithful women are punished by having an ear cut off. The man was very angry. He went to the head man and cried, 'They have punished me unfairly! Attack them! Attack the white men!'

"The head man would not attack the white men. He said, 'They are our guests. You are the one who intruded.'

"The wounded man returned full of anger to his own people and told his story. 'The white men are not to be trusted,' he said.

"His people agreed. They said if the white men came to their land, they would attack them. After a while, the white men did come. Scouts watched as they traveled by day and camped at night. When the scouts had watched for two days, they signaled the attack. Many men from their tribe came. They killed the white men and took their horses."

Fort Nez Perce, Oregon Country

Peter Ogden, chief trader with the Hudson Bay Company, checked the trapping brigade that would leave with him in the morning for an uncharted area of the Snake Country.

Short, stocky, dark-skinned Ogden was a man of calmness with dark, unwavering eyes set deep under furrowing brows. His nose, inherited from his English mother, was aristocratic. In spite of his dour-appearing mouth, he was known as a man of wit and humor.

His brigade of trappers, with their horses, traps, and supplies, appeared to be in order. He bristled again thinking of Governor Simpson's latest orders. He pictured the pompous little man and could still hear his nasal voice declaring, "And henceforth, on all future trapping expeditions, families will be left behind."

Since their marriage, Julia had accompanied him on all his trapping expeditions. His courtship of Julia and their marriage was a popular story told and retold throughout the vast northern network of Hudson Bay forts and bases. He had been stationed at the Spokane House Fort when he met Julia, an Indian princess of the Flathead tribe. She had held him at arm's length until he learned the marriage customs of her tribe. Then, on a bright, frosty morning, dressed in his London broadcloth and linen and riding a black stallion, he left the fort with a herd of fifty horses and a bevy of men. One by one, he sent his men with a horse to the lodge of Julia's mother. One by one, the horses were received by her mother. Julia did not appear. He knew by the rules of the marriage custom that she was not required to give anything in return for his gift. The forty-eighth horse was sent, and the forty-ninth, and finally his most valued—a gold-colored mare with a creamy mane and tail. He held his breath, fearing all was lost, when a cry arose from the camp observers who had been silently watching the courtship take place. There was a stir in the herd, and Julia rode out on the golden mare, resplendent in white buckskin and beadwork. Their marriage rites were completed by a ceremonial ride through the Indian encampment and around the fort.

Ogden smiled, remembering. He had no intention of leaving her behind on this trip. He had not, however, flaunted his disobedience of Simpson's order. Julia and the children and the families of his men were waiting for them a day's journey up the trail.

He slapped the hindquarters of a tethered horse. "So much for that order, O Mighty Simpson," he said aloud.

Simpson's second order was not as easy to ignore. "I have word," Simpson had announced, "that American trappers are filtering into the area. I fear they could find this region rich enough in furs to remain and lay the groundwork for American claim. Henceforth, if there is any sign of American trappers, reverse the usual trapping procedure and trap to extinction of the beaver."

The battle between the British and the Americans was not new to Ogden. His American family had backed the British during the American War for Independence. When the British lost the war, his family moved to Montreal, Canada. Growing up in Montreal, Ogden had spent hours watching boatloads of furs coming in from the wilds.

The wilds was that vast area of northern land drained by Hudson Bay, originally claimed by France. In 1608 France had begun an empire called New France with the establishment of Quebec. The economy of New France was founded on the beaver pelt. The furs were so popular in Europe that the area around Quebec was soon trapped out, and trapping was expanded into the interior. France claimed all the area that was being trapped.

In 1610 English sea captain Henry Hudson sailed into Hudson Bay while trying to find a passage to the Far East. England then claimed all land drained by the bay based on Hudson's exploration. In 1670 England's King Charles II gave the area to his cousin Prince Rupert of the Rhine and seventeen other gentlemen. In return for the king's generous land grant, the recipients were to continue looking for a Northwest Passage to the Far East and pay two elk and two beaver skins to the king each year.

As the Hudson Bay Company expanded, No. 3 Fenchurch Street in London became the Company's British headquarters, and a fort built on Hudson Bay housed the North American headquarters.

By 1763 France had been routed from the area. The Hudson Bay Company's monopoly of the fur trade was then challenged by small Canadian-Scottish companies. These companies merged in 1784, formed the Northwest Fur Company, and gained a strong foothold along the Red River of the North in the watershed of Hudson Bay.

Ogden's father had urged him to enter the field of law, but Ogden rebelled and in his early teens obtained a warehouse clerk job in the Montreal office of the upstart German-American fur merchant John Jacob Astor.

Astor had arrived in New York City from Germany when he was twenty with a few musical instruments, intending to open a music store. He soon realized the fur trade was where the money was and acquired both American and Canadian holdings. He sent a ship around South America and up the Pacific coastline to the mouth of the Columbia River. There, he established a post he named Astoria. To operate the post, Astor employed Canadian-Scottish men who were familiar with the fur trade.

In 1812, the Americans and British were again at war, and the post had no American protection. When the Canadian-Scottish employees stationed at Astoria were faced with the offer of selling out to the British Northwest Company or fighting to protect an American post, they thought it wisest to sell. The American flag came down, the British flag went up, the post was renamed Fort George, and business continued as usual sans John Jacob Astor.

Shortly after that, Ogden accepted a clerk position with the Northwest Fur Company and spent eight years at Fort Île-à-la-Crosse, three thousand miles into the Canadian wilderness, before being assigned to Fort George. Two years later, the throne of England ordered the Northwest Fur Company and the Hudson's Bay Company to stop their squabbling and merge into one company, which retained the Hudson Bay name. Ogden stayed on and worked his way up to chief trader.

Ogden had met Americans only once on a trapping expedition. American Jedediah Smith and seven of his men, employees of William Henry Ashley of Saint Louis, had arrived at the post of Spokane one December and requested permission to spend the winter. Ogden had left the following day with his trapping entourage.

One evening, late that month, the guard shouted, "Enemies!"

While every man scrambled for a gun, the approaching horsemen called out in English.

The order, "Hold your fire!" was given, and the horsemen told to proceed. As they rode into camp, the flickering firelight revealed Smith and his followers. Smith had changed his mind about wintering at the Spokane post, had trailed Ogden's party, and now requested permission to travel with them until they were out of dangerous Indian territory.

From that late-December night until the middle of March, when the weather became moderate enough to allow trapping, Smith and his men had stayed in proximity with them. After that, Ogden had been aware of where the Americans were trapping by signs and footprints until April, when the Americans had gone up the Bear River and Ogden had taken his group down.

The territory Ogden planned to cover this trip was uncharted. He hoped to find an abundance of beaver and prayed they would encounter no Americans or unfriendly Indians.

STEENS MOUNTAIN, OREGON COUNTRY

With summer, the temperature remained high. In the marshes, the ducklings were getting fat and noisy, and the old ducks were molting their flight feathers. Men on their tule rafts drove the ducks out of the water. Unable to fly, the ducks took off running on land but were unable to outrun the swift young boys. Every night the tribe feasted on baked duck. The excess kill was split open and dried.

There was rice grass to harvest, pollen from the cattails, and buckberries. Buckberry groves, found along river bottoms, were shady and cool, but their thorny, olive-green branches prevented the picking of their tart red berries by hand. Men beat the berries from the trees with sticks, allowing women and children to gather them from the ground. Some of the seed-filled berries were hand-pressed through a basketry sieve to extract the juice, and some were sun-dried for winter use.

In late summer, the circle gathered and selected scouts to search the mountain for the best crop yield of pine nuts. Pine trees could be heavy with nuts one year and produce very little the next.

When the scouts returned, each brought back a pine bough. They compared the boughs to determine the location of the best crop. A small party of men and women were then selected to visit the location and make preparations for the annual prayer dance. Early the following morning, carrying their harvesting baskets, skin water jugs, and a small supply of food to eat along the way, the group set out for the chosen pine grove.

Arriving late in the evening, they slept briefly and arose early. As the sun came up, they prayed to the Great Father, asking for good health for their people. After prayers, a fire pit was dug. One woman stayed to tend the fire while the rest gathered cones. When they returned with their baskets of cones, the woman removed the live coals from the pit, dumped the cones in, and pushed the hot earth back over the nuts. Another fire was built on top. She then threw handfuls of dirt to the north, the south, the east, and the west. Now no spirits would bring harm to the maturing crop of cones.

The people stretched out on the cool ground under the trees and slept until the woman called them to help open the green cones, remove the nuts, and store them in baskets. The nuts would be carried back to camp for everyone to eat while they participated in the prayer-dance ceremony. A small tree would also be selected and carried back to camp.

The gatherers rested a night and a day after returning to camp before the prayer-dance ceremony. The ceremony began after sunset. With shoulder touching shoulder, the people formed a tight circle around the tree that had been brought back. The tree was to show what they were dancing for. A man began to sing, and the people moved to the left with a slow, shuffling step. One after the other sang their song in the slowly moving circle.

The woman, carrying a basket of water, walked in the opposite direction around the outside of the dancers. As she prayed for rain and many nuts, she dipped a twig of sagebrush bearing a plume of tiny green sage flowers in the water and sprinkled the ground. Next she carried a basket of pine nuts around the circle, scattering them about on the ground to give back to the earth for what they had taken.

When the night was the darkest, the dancers stopped. The woman placed a helping of nuts in each outstretched hand. The dancers rested while they ate, and then the dance resumed, and the reverent circling continued until the first rays of sunshine burst over the horizon.

They rested during the day, and in the evening, the gambling hand game began. One band played against another band, the opposing bands having been picked in advance by lot. A woman began the betting with a basket she had made during the winter and carefully carried and saved for this occasion. Immediately, a woman from the other band bet a like basket. A man bet a prized rabbit-skin blanket, and the other band matched it. All went well until a young boy bet a rock he had found on the scouting trip. The other band had no rock and thus began a long process of agreeing on what they had that was comparable. Finally, a white swan feather was selected.

When all the bets were in and balanced, the two bands sat on the ground, facing each other. The bets and ten tally sticks were heaped between the two sides. In front of each group was a log on which the rhythm of songs was beat out as they sang and played the game.

The game began with a man and woman from one band, each concealing a pair of small bones within their closed hands. One bone of each pair was plain, the other ornamented. The guesser of the other band had to guess in whose hand the plain bone was hidden. If the guess was correct, that side was awarded a stick tally. If not, that side lost a tally.

The singers opposing the guesser shouted, waved, and beat the logs to cause confusion. The guesser was to concentrate, remaining oblivious to the distractions. The game continued through the night until one side had won all ten tally sticks, claiming all the prizes.

When the pine-nut celebration was over, the people went about their daily routine until the rose hips turned red. This was the signal to start moving up the mountain toward the pine-nut grove.

The departure from the warm, alkaline water of the marshes for the cooler air and cold water of the mountain springs was welcomed.

When the pine-nut grove was reached, the women built shelters of sage and pine boughs while the men hunted for sage hens, squirrels, and marmots. Children and grandparents collected wood for the evening fires. Everyone worked at gathering the cones, which had to be cleaned, roasted, ground, and packed into baskets for winter food.

Before the harvest was completed, the youngest and strongest of the people returned to the desert for the rabbit hunt. As they moved down the mountain, they watched for the fire built by the man who had been selected as rabbit-hunt captain. The fire would signify the campsite for the drive. The first to arrive sang, played games, and gambled while they waited for the others to assemble.

Every family brought a rabbit net, about three feet high, made from fiber. The nets were strung between bushes or held up with forked sticks stuck in the ground or with sagebrush pulled out by the roots and piled in rows. The rabbits were driven into the nets and killed with sticks when they became entangled in the mesh. The rabbit pelts were cut into long ribbons of fur with the use of a sharp rock. Some of the meat was eaten; the rest was dried for winter.

Rabbit drives were also courting times. To win a girl's favor, a boy brought her a duck or rabbit. If she rejected the gift, she rejected the boy. If a girl carried food or water to a boy she liked and the boy caught her wrist instead of accepting the gift, it meant he preferred the girl. Wedding negotiations were performed by grandparents, and it was the custom after marriage for the boy to go with the girl's family.

When the rabbit drive was completed, the people returned to the pine-nut location, gathered up their harvest, and headed back to the lake to make plans for the winter.

No dreams or storytellers foretold that Peter Ogden and his men were about to pay them a visit.

Chapter 2
1829

Washington, DC

It was January. The November election the previous year had gone badly for John Quincy Adams. He received the news of his defeat by Andrew Jackson with mixed feelings. Weary from the demands of office and the continual harassment by Jacksonians, he welcomed the news. On the other hand, so much of what he had hoped to accomplish was not completed.

In his inaugural address made in the Senate Chamber of the unfinished Capitol four years earlier, he had stated, "The powers of government must be used for the benefit of all the people."

This was still his belief. In his heart, he knew slavery was wrong. And he knew the slaughtering of the Indian population was wrong. Some progress had been made in that area with the establishment, under the War Department, of the Bureau of Indian Affairs. But the masses of European-Americans were still pressing into any and all unclaimed areas while Jackson supporters shouted, "Let the people rule!"

As for slavery, he would continue to fight it as an institution. He hoped the rumors he had heard were true and he would be asked to run for Congress in 1830.

This morning he sat behind his desk in his upstairs study in the

White House. It was the beginning of a new year, and he repeated to himself, "The powers of government must be used for the benefit of all the people."

He glanced at the clock on the wall. His assistant would soon be in, and today they must work out arrangements for a meeting with president-elect Jackson. He hoped to make the transition of office as smoothly as possible, regardless of differing beliefs and feelings. A few moments later, however, his plans were shattered when his assistant entered the room and delivered an unexpected message.

"Mrs. Jackson has died," he said. "She suffered a heart attack on December 22 at their home in Nashville and died that evening."

"I'm sorry," Adams answered. "We must send condolences immediately."

"Mr. President, there is more to the message. Jackson is laying the blame of his wife's death on the shoulders of you and your campaigners. He claims his wife died of a broken heart because of the humiliation you caused her to suffer. He says you are murderers he can never forgive."

Adams bowed his head and covered his face with his hands. All during his tenure in office, Jackson and his supporters had done their best to embarrass him with their continued taunts of "bargain," "corruption," and "usurpation." Mudslinging, to him, was disgraceful, and he had refrained from retaliating. He was aware, however, that his supporters had responded to the Jacksonian word battle by making Jackson's marriage a campaign issue.

Thirty-seven years earlier, Jackson and Mrs. Rachel Robards had married, believing her husband had obtained a divorce. Two years later, they learned their wedding had taken place a month before the divorce had actually been granted to Capt. Robards. Upon learning this, they immediately repeated their marriage vows. When this information surfaced during the campaign, Jackson was called a "paramour husband" and Mrs. Jackson a "convicted adulteress."

Adams raised his head, sighed, leaned back in his chair, and said to his assistant, "Is that all?"

"No, sir, there is more. Jackson sent word he does not intend to meet with you before the inauguration or after."

Adams felt the sting and immediately replied with one of his own: "Then I will not attend the inauguration. We will leave the White House the day before."

FORT VANCOUVER, OREGON COUNTRY

It was late in July. Three days earlier, Peter Ogden had parted from Julia; she and the children would go on to Fort Nez Perce, and he to Fort Vancouver. Now he stood on the wooden porch of the home of Dr. John McLoughlin, chief factor of the Hudson Bay Company's Columbia District, waiting for the dinner bell to ring. The ten-room home, with its white picket fence surrounding abundant flowers, seemed like a palatial oasis.

From the porch, Ogden surveyed the fort, enclosed by a stockade twenty feet high. Two cannons were mounted on the lawn in front of the porch. In addition to McLoughlin's residence and those of the officers, forty or so other buildings lay within the stockade. There was the chapel, the pharmacy, and the separate workshops for mechanics, carpenters, blacksmiths, coopers, wheelwrights, and tanners. Behind the buildings was a large vegetable garden and a fruit orchard. Only the area within the stockade was considered the fort. Two wide double gates, locked and guarded by kilted sentries, served as entrance and exit points for wagons and carts.

Outside the stockade, on the bank of the Columbia River, was a village of houses built in rows so as to form streets. Fields outside the stockade, planted with wheat, peas, and potatoes, also served as pasturage for sheep, horses, and cattle. The fields made the post self-sustaining and also produced enough to furnish the company's subsidiary fur posts with some of their needed foodstuffs.

The fort had grown considerably since the sunrise ceremony on March 19, 1825, when Governor Simpson had broken a bottle of rum on the flag staff and christened the newly-built Fort Vancouver as headquarters of the Columbia District.

After the British acquired Fort Astoria in 1812 and renamed it Fort George, it continued as a strategic post until Dr. McLoughlin's arrival in 1824 to take command of the Columbia District. McLoughlin, born in 1784 in Quebec, was a mixture of Irish, Scotch, and French-Canadian blood. As a youth, he had received training in medicine, becoming licensed to practice medicine and surgery by the age of nineteen. He was hired by the Northwest Fur Company as a physician but soon became a trader with the company. In 1821 he was sent to London as one of the company's representatives to arrange for the merger with the rival Hudson Bay Company. Within three years, he received his appointment as chief factor for the Columbia District.

Governor Simpson had accompanied McLoughlin to Fort George in 1824. The two men soon determined the location was not suitable as headquarters for the district, and the new location, ninety miles up the Columbia River, near the confluence of the Columbia and Willamette Rivers, was selected.

Ogden pictured the dining hall of Dr. McLoughlin's home. He had sat before at its huge mahogany dining table set with damask napery, flat silver, Waterford glassware, and Spode china and been served multicourse gourmet dinners prepared by servants in the kitchen located behind the main house. Perhaps today there would be vegetable soup; rice; a variety of meats and fish; fresh bread and hot biscuits; puddings; melons; grapes; and cheese.

The dinner bell rang. Ogden took a deep breath, turned, and walked into the house. It was good to be back in civilization.

The meal was as bountiful as he had imagined. He savored each bite while listening to the conversation of the other men at the table. McLoughlin, seated at the head of the table, was an imposing figure more than six feet tall, with piercing eyes and prematurely white hair hanging down over massive shoulders. James Douglas, heir apparent to McLoughlin's position, was there along with the captain of a supply vessel from London, three visiting chief factors, and Tom McKay, McLoughlin's stepson.

The conversation centered around Governor Simpson's winter visit, which had strangely coincided with the stay of the American trapper Jedediah Smith. Ogden listened with interest to the story of Smith's arriving at the fort after being set upon by Indians and how McLoughlin had immediately assembled a forty-man party to accompany Smith back to the scene of the attack. The party had retrieved a few mules, about five hundred beaver skins, and various odds and ends: rifles, pistols, traps, and a few cooking kettles.

Smith and his three men had returned to the fort with the rescue party and spent the winter there. While the retrieval mission was going on, Governor Simpson had arrived at the fort, also planning to spend the winter.

Simpson and the American Smith as winter guests, Ogden thought to himself. *The doctor must have had his hands full.*

When the meal was over, the men retired to the Bachelor's Hall for smoking and wine. Now it was Ogden's turn to talk.

"Well, Peter," McLoughlin said, raising his wine glass, "Tell us where you've been and what you've seen."

"As you know," Ogden began, "I left Fort Nez Perce on the twenty-second of September without my family, per the governor's instructions."

No point, Ogden thought, explaining how Julia and the children had gone on ahead and waited for him a day's journey up the trail. If McLoughlin had heard of it, he was too much of a gentleman to bring it up.

"My party was well supplied with horses and traps, but some of the horses were unseasoned, and on the second day, nine of them gave out in the Blue Mountains."

McLoughlin shook his head. Simpson's corner cutting, which often resulted in inferior outfitting, disgusted him.

"We stayed in the Grand Ronde Valley for two days, making tent poles, and then crossed the Grande Ronde River to the Powder River. I divided the party there." Ogden stopped for a moment and dramatically wiped his brow. "I found the temperature hard to believe. End of September, and hotter than the middle of July!"

The men chuckled, nodded, and sipped their wine. Ogden continued, "I sent six men on down to Burnt River and another five across country with the instruction to trap wherever they found beaver and meet us at the Malheur River. Payette stayed with me a couple more days, and then I sent him and his party off to trap the north and south branches. I gave Payette a small trading assortment in case he ran into any Americans."

Young McKay uncrossed his legs and leaned forward in his chair. He was eager to continue the talk about Jedediah Smith, and the mention of Americans gave him an opening.

McLoughlin, however, held up a paternal hand and silenced him. He was fond of his stepson, but McKay was known for monopolizing the conversation, and the rest of the evening belonged to Ogden.

Ogden nodded to McKay and continued his report. "I got to the Malheur River the next afternoon, expecting to be met by a Snake Indian guide. He never showed. A few days later, the Burnt River party showed up. Trapping had been light, and eight of their horses had been stolen. We suspected Shoshone but found no sign of a band or the horses.

"By the middle of October, our party was again intact, and we struck out across unexplored country until we came to a lake. The lake was lined with wretched huts shared by half-naked savages. I tried every way I knew how to question them about the country but couldn't make them understand. It was obvious they had never seen white men before."

Ogden stopped for a moment and closed his eyes, remembering how frightened the people had appeared. He had wanted to give them something to allay their fear. When he had reached into his satchel, his hand had fallen upon a looking glass, which they had accepted with amazement. Quickly clearing his mind, he opened his eyes and continued. His report, of course, was on beaver, not Indians.

"We continued our exploring. We found a series of lakes, which I named River of Lakes. We camped on one of the lakes and fanned out to explore the area. Less than four miles from our camp, I caught sight of a large stream appearing from nowhere and flowing east between banks covered with willows. I made all speed to reach it, and the first thing I saw was a beaver house well stocked!"

Ogden continued with his tale of successful trapping. A thousand beaver were taken before snow closed the season. "We were breaking camp to move south," he continued, "when Joseph Paul stumbled into camp, near dead. It was the general opinion that Paul would not survive, but God forbid we should hasten his death, so we decided to stay in camp a few days to allow him rest and care.

"But," Ogden continued, "Paul didn't respond, and with provisions running low, I had no choice but to move on. I took every precaution to have him well covered with robes and blankets. I assigned two men to assist him and lead his horse. All went well the first day. The second day, the trail was hilly and the snow two feet deep. We made camp at three in the afternoon and shortly after, one of the men in charge of Paul rode in with the news that Paul's horse had given out. I immediately sent aid, and at about seven in the evening, they brought Paul into camp. By the next morning, his pain was nearly unbearable, and he begged me to go on without him. That I could not do, but two of my men came forward and volunteered to remain behind with him.

"While I was pondering their proposal, an older Indian entered camp and approached me. If he had been frightened at first, he had overcome his fear and was able to communicate that in exchange for a horse, he would guide us out of the snow area. I gave him a three-year-old colt and a bag of peas, and a week later, true to his word, we were out of the snow area and close to Salt Lake. Our guide, no doubt feeling his part of the bargain was accomplished, disappeared that night. One of my men shot an antelope, and a few days later, a couple of buffalo were killed. That, along with killing and eating a horse that was dying, revived the strength of the party.

"On New Year's Day, one of the men left behind with Paul came into camp and reported that Paul had died eight days after we left. They gave him a decent burial."

The group in the room murmured their condolences. Joseph Paul had been well liked. He had been a member of the Northwest Fur Company's first Snake expedition in 1819. A steady young man, he had won recognition as one of the best trappers in the country.

"The other man had fallen behind, so I sent a man and two horses to rescue him. The news of Paul gave me no heart for a New Year's celebration, so I delayed it for three days. On the third of January, I gave each man a dram of spirits and a foot of tobacco.

"The next three months, we camped and scoured the country around Salt Lake. We found enough food to keep going, but few beaver. The Indians we ran into were hostile, killing one of my men in Weber Canyon.

"In April we started west, ending up at Unknown River. Some of my trappers had gone on ahead and taken quite a catch of beaver. After exhausting the beaver in the Unknown River, we went on in a northwesterly direction. The Indians we encountered had no guns but had swift horses and deadly aim with their arrows. Even though I instructed my trappers to go out only in twos and be strictly on their guard, traps were stolen, and two men barely escaped with their lives. On June 2, having reached our goal of two thousand furs, we directed our course homeward and, by the grace of God Almighty, here I am."

The men continued on with questions until McLoughlin rose and extended his hand to Ogden. "Well done, as usual. Your room is ready. I expect you want to retire for the night."

RENDEZVOUS, PIERRE'S HOLE

Jedediah Smith had left Fort Vancouver in the spring bound for Pierre's Hole at the western base of the Teton mountain range. Scattered throughout the Rockies were numerous small, protected valleys where trappers spent their winters. Smith was confident that if he could reach Pierre's Hole in time, he could get information on Rendezvous.

Rendezvous, developed by William Ashley, had been the annual meeting of trappers and traders for the past four years, and Smith had no reason to believe there would not be another one held this year. When American trappers had first begun trapping the wilds, Saint Louis was the only place they could deliver their furs and buy supplies for the next season. In 1824 Ashley had preselected the site of Henry's Fork on the Green River and told his men he would be there the following spring prepared to buy and transport their furs back to Saint Louis. He would also have supplies for them to buy. Supplies would include, in addition to traps and necessary gear, trinkets for Indian barter, tobacco, coffee, and alcohol.

Smith had attended first Rendezvous. Over one hundred trappers met, plus friendly Indians and their families. Except for an attack from the Blackfeet Indians, who were routed with no casualties, everything went smoothly. It had been a genuine, friendly social affair that culminated with his becoming a fifty-fifty partner with Ashley, replacing Andrew Henry, who was quitting the mountain life.

At the second Rendezvous, held on the Snake River, Ashley had sold his half of the business to David Jackson and William Sublette, but furnished the supplies for third Rendezvous, held on the Bear River. Smith had been in California and had missed fourth Rendezvous, when William Sublette was to take over delivery of supplies. Smith had contacted no one in the past year who could give him information on what had transpired.

Smith carried with him a draft for $2,400, payment received at Fort Vancouver for the few furs salvaged from the Indian attack. If he reached Rendezvous, he would use the money for supplies to outfit his next trapping expedition. McLoughlin had paid him top price for his furs, even though the furs would not have been recovered without the aid of McLoughlin.

Smith thought about McLoughlin—a good man. He had found Simpson barely tolerable, but McLoughlin had treated him like royalty throughout the entire winter and sternly refused every offer of compensation for his hospitality. Perhaps, Smith thought, he could still repay him if he could influence the American trappers to trap the east side of the Rockies and leave the west side to the Hudson Bay Company.

Smith was surprised when he reached Pierre's Hole to find about 175 men waiting for the supply train to arrive. He was warmly greeted. Everyone had thought him dead when he failed to show up at Rendezvous the previous year. He was told William Sublette had delivered supplies the year before and had told them to meet him at Pierre's Hole the next year. They now had their tents pitched in the valley and were becoming more impatient every day waiting for him to arrive. To pass the time, Smith told and retold his stories of California and of his dealings with Mexican authorities, of the Indian attack, and of spending the winter at Fort Vancouver.

It was August 20 before Sublette and his supply train rolled into the valley. Sublette had left Saint Louis with the supplies and fifty-five men a few days before Smith had left Fort Vancouver. However, Sublette had gone first to meet some of the trappers at the

Popo Agie River and then gone on to Jackson Hole before coming to Pierre's Hole.

The men quickly forgave him, however, as the alcohol was distributed. Each year the number of people attending Rendezvous had increased, and the socializing had grown wilder. Smith watched with regret as this year's rowdiness reached an all-time high.

CHAPTER 3

1830

CALIFORNIA

Ewing Young and Peter Ogden met unexpectedly in the San Joaquin Valley in California. It was an amiable meeting, and for ten days the British and the Americans traveled together, enjoying each other's company and sharing stories in a common language of their more or less hostile treatment by Spanish-Mexicans.

The year before, Young's health had improved, and he had recruited three trappers to go with him to the Gila River. They had reached the river in good time, found a trapper's dream, set up camp, and begun trapping. At first Young felt they were being observed from the brush along the river and kept an around-the-clock vigil. As the days and nights passed and no Indians were sighted, he relaxed their guard, and the men concentrated on trapping, scraping, stretching, and drying the beaver pelts.

The Apaches struck the morning Young and his men were packed and ready to start for home. They had mounted their horses to move out when the Indians swarmed from the brush. To save their lives, there was nothing they could do but ride off at dead speed, leaving the pack animals, the furs, and all their equipment behind.

"I'll be back," Young had vowed. "I'll be back to even the score!"

In Taos, he had spent time with Maria, but his focus was on returning to the Gila. This time he would go prepared. He recruited forty of the toughest mountain men he could find. He wanted to make sure he had enough men and guns along to hold off any attack the Apaches threw at him.

Just before he left, Kit Carson returned and looked him up.

"You back to learn the trappin' business?" Young asked.

"Yes, sir," Carson replied.

"Good. I'll take you along as camp boy."

Carson, hiding his disappointment, accepted Young's offer.

Trapping on the Gila was successful. The increased man and gunpower kept the Apaches at bay. During the first scrimmage, Kit Carson proved to be the best shot in the outfit. After the Apaches had been routed, Carson cut his first notch in his rifle stock, and Young graduated him from camp boy to trapper.

In no time, they reached their limit of furs and were ready to return to Taos. That night Young lay awake, thinking first of Maria and then of California. It was still early in the season. He had his passport. He was halfway to California. Should he continue on or return to Taos and wait another year?

By morning he had made his decision. He split the party and sent half of his men with the furs back to Taos by a more southerly route to avoid the Apaches. With Kit Carson and the rest of his men, he set out for California.

After crossing two desert areas, carrying drinking water in deer-hide bags, and surviving on dried jerky made from shredded deer meat, they reached Mission San Gabriel. They were not openly attacked at the mission, but neither was there a welcoming party to greet them.

Mission San Gabriel was one of twenty-one missions built over a period of fifty-four years from 1769 to 1823 by Spanish Franciscans. Spain's claim to California was based on Spanish explorers who had sailed up and down the coast in the 1600s. Lower California was settled shortly after that, but no attempt was made to settle Upper California for another 160 years—not until Russian ships began landing on the coast of California to collect skins of otters and seals.

Spain's decision to hold the land and keep the Russians out coincided with the dream of a Franciscan friar born on the island of Majorca, near the coast of Spain. As a boy attending a convent school there, Father Junipero Serra had heard of California and longed to go there to teach and help the Indians. His wish was granted, and he had been teaching in Lower California for twenty years when he was chosen to be head of missions in Upper California.

The king of Spain wanted four things to be accomplished in Upper California: he wanted missions built; he wanted the land held for Spain; he wanted other countries kept out; and he wanted a seaport built that would accommodate ocean-sailing vessels.

Father Serra oversaw the building of the first mission at San Diego in 1769. The second mission built was San Carlos, on Monterey Bay. Other missions, a day's journey apart, were built between the two and on up the coastline to San Francisco.

The Indians in the area responded to the intruders in different ways. Some resisted; others came to the missions and lived there, learning how to care for the herds of cattle, horses, and sheep brought up from Mexico. They learned how to grow and harvest grain and corn and grapes, and they learned the Christian religion.

Once the missions were established, settlers from Mexico began moving into the area, bringing with them their celebration customs and their lifestyle.

The antagonism Young and his party felt when they reached Mission San Gabriel caused them to push on after only a day's rest. They went north, toward San Francisco Bay, trapping as they went. When they reached Mission San Jose, they found the Catholic fathers in charge of the mission very upset. Native Indians had stolen a herd of horses. It was the second herd stolen within the year. Kit Carson volunteered to go in pursuit. Apprehensively, Young agreed to let him go and sent ten men with him.

Three days later, Carson and the men returned with the herd intact. The fathers showed their appreciation by outfitting Young with well-shod horses, mules, and supplies.

Determined to see as much of California as he could, Young continued on, and when they reached San Joaquin Valley and found signs that another trapping party had recently been in the area, they hurried to overtake them. The party turned out to be Peter Ogden's Hudson Bay trappers.

It was Ogden's sixth trapping season, and the season had not been as successful as prior years. After spending a few days at Fort Vancouver the year before, he had traveled on to Fort Nez Perce and spent the summer with Julia and the children before leaving in the fall for the Salt Lake region.

He and Julia had sent their oldest son, ten-year-old Peter, east to Alexander Ross's school at Red River Settlement. They had then agreed that Julia and the other children would remain with her mother at Fort Nez Perce for the trapping season.

Finding beaver nearly extinct in his usual trapping areas, Ogden went east of the High Sierras into Mexican territory and trapped on up to the San Joaquin Valley. He was there able to increase his catch to one thousand pelts and was drifting north toward Oregon when Ewing Young's party caught up with him.

When the two groups reached the foothills of the Siskiyou Mountains, they parted. Ogden continued north, toward Fort Vancouver, and Young went south, toward the little village of Los Angeles.

Fort Vancouver

When Ogden reached Fort Vancouver in October, he was near his breaking point. Disaster had struck on the Columbia River. When they had reached the river, nine of his trappers had loaded the furs on a boat to glide downstream to their intended camp for the night. Ogden elected to walk down along the riverbank. Scarcely had the men pushed off before the boat was caught in a huge whirlpool of water that pulled the boat under. Only one man escaped from the whirling vortex of water.

When Ogden reached Fort Vancouver, exhausted and grief-stricken, he found that malaria had struck the entire valley. It had begun with a few servants complaining of fever who did not respond to the usual remedies. Within twenty days, the fever had spread through the entire garrison. Dr. McLoughlin turned the fort into a hospital and sent word to the nearby Indians of how to deal with the fever. As far as they could tell, the epidemic had been brought by crew members aboard a ship from New England that had come up the river and anchored near the fort.

Ogden was also stricken, and a month passed before he recovered sufficiently to be back on his feet. As soon as he was able, he set out with a party of other convalescing men for the nearest Indian village. They found only dead bodies. The Indians had not followed McLoughlin's instructions but had used their own remedy for fever, which was plunging into cold water. The illness proved fatal for three-fourths of the Indian population in the valley.

The one bit of good news Ogden received was that Governor Simpson had found a replacement for him, and he was to go on no more trapping expeditions. His new assignment was to travel north, by ship, and establish an Indian trading post on the Nass River. The trading post was intended to compete with American traders whose method of trading was to sail up the coast and anchor offshore in bay areas. The Indians would canoe out to them and barter their furs for articles. Simpson's plan was for Ogden to build and reside at a fort on the Nass River. When word came of an American ship in the area, he was to take a vessel loaded with articles, anchor near the American ship, and offer the Indians better prices for their furs than the Americans did.

Ogden, dubious the plan would drive the Americans out of the area, nevertheless looked forward, after his years of wandering, to having a permanent home with his family around him. He sent word to Julia to remain at Fort Nez Perce. He would spend the winter recuperating at Fort Vancouver. In the spring, they would reunite on the Nass River.

CHAPTER 4
1831

BOSTON

Hall Jackson Kelley, Bostonian ex-teacher, gripped his pen and wrote with passion.

"Mountains are high and rough. The air is more salubrious, and the country better furnished with natural facilities for application of labour.

"The settlement of the Oregon Country would conduce to a freer intercourse, and a more extensive and lucrative trade with the East Indias."

Oregon! If only he could see it for himself! He had eagerly searched out and read everything written about the country. He closed his eyes, trying to picture the lofty mountains, the rushing rivers, the verdant valleys. Then a familiar wave of anger swept over him. He opened his eyes and banged his fist on the table. Why didn't the government do something to encourage Americans to settle the Oregon Country? Didn't they realize how the British were expanding their operations?

A reckless thought came to him. *Hang waiting for the government to do something! If other people knew what I know about Oregon, they would flock there.* He would form an Oregon Colonization

Society, invite people to meetings, and tell them about Oregon. Oregon for Americans!

In the days that followed, he posted notices. He ran an ad in the newspaper. The meetings, however, were sparsely attended. Those who came left without showing any interest in colonizing Oregon.

Kelley persisted, and one evening, as he finished speaking, a man came forward. The tall, slender man looked comparatively young in spite of his thinning hair.

Kelley held out his hand, which was gripped in a firm handshake.

"I'm Nathaniel Wyeth," the man said. "I'm interested in going to Oregon."

Kelley was overjoyed. At last! A recruit!

Nathaniel Wyeth, thirty years old, was an ice merchant in Cambridge, Massachusetts. He boasted an impressively American heritage, being related to John Hancock of Massachusetts on his mother's side and to George Wyeth of Virginia on his father's (both men signers of the Declaration of Independence). Adding more credence to his heritage, his father was a graduate of Harvard University.

Wyeth sifted through the information Kelley gave him, not as a colonizer, but with the eye of a businessman. Soon he was telling other young Massachusetts merchants, "I believe there's a fortune to be made in Oregon in fur and salmon trade."

FORT GIBSON, INDIAN TERRITORY

Capt. Benjamin Bonneville paced the wooden floor of his austere office at Fort Gibson, the Army outpost on the newly formed Cherokee Indian Territory. The movement of tribes from their lands in the south to new land west of the Mississippi River was progressing. Now that Andrew Jackson was president, Bonneville knew the task would soon be completed. His pacing, however, was not over the movement of the Cherokee. It was his own movement that concerned him. His request for a leave of absence to explore the West had been granted. At times like this, he wondered if his insatiable curiosity was a blessing or a curse.

He had left the comforts of France, his birthplace, to come to America, where his admittance to West Point had been arranged. His duties at frontier army posts after graduating were pleasantly interrupted when Marquis de Lafayette returned to America for a visit and Bonneville was selected to serve as his aide. The aide service continued when Lafayette returned to France. Bonneville, despite feeling more than welcome in Lafayette's grand home, once again chose America and returned to his Army life.

Now, at the age of thirty-eight, alone at Fort Gibson following the death of his young wife and infant baby, he had begun looking longingly West, imagining what lay beyond his vision—until one day an idea came to mind: a leave of absence for exploration purposes. Before submitting his request, he thought it through with great care. He would request a two-year leave, stressing, first and foremost, that the leave would be of a personal nature, undertaken for immediate profit in the fur business. Second, such leave would allow for his personal exploration of uncharted American lands to determine topography and the numbers and kinds of Natives living in the land; examine the nature of the English establishment in Oregon; and possibly obtain information on the Spanish/Mexican settlements in California. Such information, of course, would be obtained for possible future personal business endeavors for profit. However, he would furnish the government with a complete report of his exploration upon his return.

He would point out that few men were blessed with more influential friends than he. These friends, he would suggest, might be disposed to financing a personal adventure of this type.

He dispatched his written proposal. More quickly than he had anticipated, he received word back from the government that his request for leave had been approved and that his exploration of the country to the Rocky Mountains and beyond would receive complete financial backing from a group of Manhattan businessmen.

Upon receiving approval of his request, Bonneville immediately began recruiting men and equipment. There was no lack of men eager to accompany him into the wilds, and the financing received was sufficient to purchase the best of equipment. Still, today, back and forth he paced, occasionally reaching into his pocket for a handkerchief to wipe the perspiration from his face and forehead up to his receding hairline.

Finally, in frustration, he put the question bothering him into words. "How," he said aloud, "will I find my way through the treacherous, unmapped mountains?"

No sooner had he voiced the question than a young corporal appeared in the doorway and in military fashion announced, "Sir! A trader who gives his name as Joseph Walker requests permission to meet with you!"

"Walker? Joe Walker?" A gleam appeared in Bonneville's eyes, and a smile played around his mouth. Joseph Walker—sheriff of Jackson County, Missouri! Perhaps this was his answer. He said to the corporal, "Escort Mr. Walker in at once."

When Walker entered the room, Bonneville noticed first his firm mouth, graceful nose, and unwavering eyes. Walker was also big and handsome, with black shoulder-length hair, a full beard, and a mustache.

Bonneville extended his hand and unconsciously nodded his head as reports he had heard of Walker came to mind: A good lawman. Keeps order with his imposing presence. Seldom draws his gun, but when he does, his aim is deadly. Wilderness experience.

"Good to meet you, Sheriff Walker," Bonneville said.

Walker smiled. "You can drop the title. I've resigned as sheriff. I'm here to buy horses and cattle."

Joseph Walker, born in the Tennessee Mountains, had gone west to Missouri in 1818. The Walkers of his ancestry had been Presbyterian Scotch Irish who immigrated to Pennsylvania from Ulster in the early 1700s, and then from there to the Appalachians. The next generation had gone on to the Tennessee frontier. He was related by blood and marriage to nearly everyone else in Tennessee: the Pooges, Paxtons, Pattersons, Toomys, Coulters, Youngs, Martins, Moores, Houstons, Carsons.

When Walker was fifteen, Army recruiters had come through looking for young men to aid Andrew Jackson in putting down a Creek rebellion led by William Weatherford, son of a Creek mother and Scotch Irish father. He and his older brother Joel, who was sixteen, joined the regiment and were with Jackson when the Creeks were defeated at Horseshoe Bend. Sam Houston was the first to storm their barricade, and Joel was slightly wounded when he followed.

When the brothers were released from service four years later, they returned to Tennessee and then moved with their family to Fort Osage in Missouri. The family selected an available tract of heavily timbered land west of the government post, cleared the land, and used the trees for putting up buildings.

By 1820, the buildings, including a smith shop, were finished. A crop of corn had been planted, along with apple trees brought from Tennessee. The two brothers, feeling the family could now manage without them, set off to explore the country.

Joel returned to Missouri the following year, but Joe went on to Santa Fe with a caravan carrying trade goods. In 1824 he was commissioned by the federal government to join a survey team that mapped and marked part of the Santa Fe route. Three years after that, he accepted the position of first sheriff of Jackson County.

Independence, the county seat, was a wide-open Western boomtown that needed taming. He had done his best, but when his four-year term was up, he was anxious to move on; he turned in his badge. A horse and cattle buying trip had brought him to Fort Gibson.

Bonneville decided very soon, as they exchanged conversation, that Walker was indeed the answer to his dilemma. He offered Walker the position of field commander for his upcoming Western venture. Walker accepted. They parted, agreeing to meet at Fort Osage, ten miles from Independence, in early spring.

TAOS, NEW MEXICO

Ewing Young prepared with sadness to return to California. When he came home to Taos in April, he found he had been gone too long. While he was away, Maria had given birth to their son, Jose Joaquin Young. All she had known was that he had sent half of his men home from the Gila and left for California with the other half.

Her love for him had grown cold as she waited, not knowing when or if he would come back.

He and Kit Carson went on to Santa Fe and met David Jackson, William Sublette, and Thomas Fitzpatrick. Fitzpatrick was taking a supply train to Rendezvous and hired Carson to accompany him.

Jackson and Sublette listened with interest to Young's stories of his California travels. When he told about the great numbers of livestock he had seen on the mission ranches, they agreed that if they could find a route that would sustain livestock, they could make a fortune running cattle from California to Missouri.

Convinced a suitable route could be found, Jackson left for California in August. When Sublette left to return to Missouri, Young returned to Taos to try once more to reconcile with Maria. He found her no more receptive than he had in April. When he suggested he might return to California, she did not protest. It was time to say good-bye.

CHAPTER 5

1832

═══════════════════════════════════════

INDEPENDENCE, MISSOURI

The hubbub of Independence, Missouri, bore no resemblance to Boston and even less to Cambridge. Nathaniel Wyeth's men were anxious to be out of there as soon as possible, and Wyeth immediately began making inquiries for a guide.

Wyeth had worked diligently since his meeting with Hall Kelley the year prior. His mind had focused on Oregon day and night. He designed three wagons, including one in the shape of a boat mounted on large wagon wheels that he believed would serve as a dual vehicle for crossing the prairies and floating down rivers. Small supplies and trade items were carried in the wagons. For transporting heavy goods, he raised money and outfitted a ship that was on its way around the Horn and up the western coastline to the mouth of the Columbia River. He and twenty-four other adventurers were now on their way by land, planning to meet the ship when it arrived. They had said good-bye to their families on March 11 and headed out.

Hall Kelley had requested passage with them to Oregon, but when the time came to leave, Kelley was in Washington, DC, presenting a petition to Congress. Anxious to be off, Wyeth had left without him.

Not until they reached Saint Louis did Wyeth learn how fierce competition in the fur business had become. He also learned the wagons he had personally designed were completely unsuitable for the western terrain. Undaunted, he sold or traded his large wagons for smaller wagons and spoke convincingly to his men. "We can't compete in the fur business," he told them, "but there is still a fortune to be made in the salmon-pickling business."

Three men were unconvinced and turned back. He and the other twenty-one continued on under clear skies to Independence. Once Wyeth arrived there, his question for a guide was answered by a man who told him, "Go on across town. William Sublette is getting a supply train ready for Rendezvous."

"Rendezvous?" Wyeth repeated.

"Pierre's Hole. Rocky Mountains."

Wyeth hesitated. "We are going to Oregon. This man, William Sublette ... does he know the West?"

"Sublette's been west more times than anyone round here. What he ain't seen, he saw through the eyes of his partner."

"And who might his partner be?"

"Jedediah Smith."

Wyeth had heard of Smith. He set out across town immediately. He found Sublette lashing down a supply wagon.

"Mr. Sublette?" he said, extending his hand. "I'm Nathaniel Wyeth of Massachusetts. My men and I are heading for Oregon. I've read your partner's report on the country."

Sublette shook his hand and raised a quizzical eyebrow.

"The report your partner Jedediah Smith wrote for the government after he spent the winter at Fort Vancouver," Wyeth clarified.

Sublette nodded.

"How is Mr. Smith?" Wyeth asked.

"Dead," Sublette answered.

Wyeth drew back in shock and surprise.

"Happened a year ago," Sublette went on. "We'd sold out our trappin' company and were fixin' to take a load of supplies on down to Santa Fe. Jed went ridin' on ahead, lookin' for a water hole, and got hisself killed by a horde of screamin' Comanches."

Wyeth dropped the subject. "Like I said, my men and I are bound for Oregon. I'm wondering if we can ride along with you."

"Can as far as I go. Pierre's Hole. Might be you can hook up there with my brother Milton."

Wyeth weighed the alternatives: leave with Sublette for Pierre's Hole, wherever that was, and take a chance on getting an escort from there to Oregon, or wait and hope a train going all the way to Oregon would form before summer.

"Know of any more trains forming?" he asked.

"Nope. A twenty-wagon train led by Capt. Bonneville headed out in April. Bonneville claimed he was takin' a leave from the Army to do some trappin'. Didn't believe him. Could tell he was no trapper. Had a good guide with him, though—Joe Walker."

"How soon are you leaving?" Wyeth asked.

"Day after tomorrow."

Wyeth nodded. He had made up his mind. "We'll be ready," he said. "Don't leave without us." He turned and went back to prepare his men.

NEW ORLEANS

Hall J. Kelley stepped off the boat in New Orleans, alone. He had returned to Boston from Washington in May and immediately inquired about Nathaniel Wyeth. With disbelief, shock, and anger, he discovered Wyeth and his group had gone west without him.

"It's time," Kelley had shouted to the few men gathered at his Oregon Colonization Society meeting. "It's time Hall Kelley finds his own way to Oregon! Who will go with me?"

Kelley outlined his plan, and a few men began to show interest. They would travel as a loose-knit group, he explained, each man responsible for his own provisions. He promised complete safety in crossing the settled area of America to Independence, Missouri. Chances were good they would arrive in time to catch Wyeth there. If so, they would join him for the remainder of the trip. If Wyeth had already left and could not reasonably be overtaken, there was boat passage available to New Orleans. From New Orleans, they would strike west across American-settled Mexican territory to

California. From California, they would press north and follow the coastline to Oregon.

Four men agreed to accompany him, and Kelley hastily made plans to be off. They reached Independence without incident but found Wyeth's group had already left. Upon receiving this information, the four men from Boston turned back. Kelley, determined, booked passage alone on the first boat he could get to New Orleans.

He was not concerned about the lateness of the season. The weather in the south would not contain the winter hazards of the upland plains and mountains. Perhaps, too, it was as well he traveled alone. One man would attract less suspicion than a group of travelers. He had heard that relations between the American settlers and Mexican officials were growing steadily worse.

In 1820, Moses Austin, a Missouri banker, had made a deal with the Spanish government to establish an American colony in Texas. The colonists were to embrace the Catholic Church and the Spanish government. Austin died before he could organize the colony, but his son Stephen Austin carried out the plan by bringing three hundred American families to Texas.

In a few years, the number of American settlers grew to upward of 25,000. By then Mexico had gained its independence from Spain. Mexican officials, alarmed by the increasing number of settlers, in 1830 halted all further American immigration to Texas.

This did not stop Kelley. He was on his way to Oregon, he reasoned. Just passing through.

SNAKE RIVER

Nathaniel Wyeth and his handful of remaining men waited at the Snake River in anticipation of the arrival of friendly Indians who were to escort them across the Blue Mountains to the Columbia River.

They had left Independence on May 12 in the company of William Sublette's group. Sublette demanded a grueling twenty-five miles a day. The men lacked good water. Food was scarce. Fourteen more of Wyeth's men turned back. On July 7, the remaining men crossed the divide and looked down at the rendezvous camp spread out in the valley below.

Pierre's Hole, about thirty miles in length and fifteen in width, was bounded by a low, broken ridge and overlooked by distant lofty mountains called the Tetons. A stream fed by mountain springs flowed through the valley toward the north, dividing it in half. Meadows, broad and extensive, were dotted with groves of willow and cottonwood trees.

The serenity of the scene changed drastically as they dropped down into the valley. At least two hundred traders, trappers, and hunters, both Indian and white, had pitched their tents and were celebrating with wild stories, gambling, and horse racing. When Sublette's supply train distributed the eagerly awaited alcohol, the celebrating grew more riotous and continued through the night. Some of Wyeth's remaining Bostonians had no stomach for the celebrating and, in spite of his entreaties, left in the morning to return home.

Wyeth selected an area beyond the main encampment and set up camp. William Sublette introduced him to his brother, Milton, who agreed they could ride with him as far as the Snake River, and he would arrange for an escort to meet them there.

Ten days passed before Milton Sublette and his men were ready to travel. Wyeth took the opportunity to roam the valley. He was totally impressed by the competition in the fur trade. Gathered in the valley were men from the American Fur Company, the Hudson Bay Company, the Rocky Mountain Company, and other smaller independent companies.

Wyeth found Milton Sublette more congenial than his brother. When they reached the Snake River, they parted by shaking hands warmly, and Wyeth said with true sincerity, "Wish you were going on with us."

"No trapping left where you're going," Sublette said. "We're heading for a place called the Humboldt. Wish us luck!"

Humboldt Lake

Milton Sublette and his men broke camp early in November and moved on. After leaving Wyeth at the Snake River in August, they had trailed in a generally southwesterly direction and reached the Humboldt area in the first part of October. Food was plentiful, so they made no effort to contact the Indians, who scattered and hid from them as they passed through.

After skirting the headwaters of the Humboldt for a month, Sublette, anxious to see more of the country to the south, elected to move on. He calculated that wintering farther south would give his men a jump start on spring trapping while they worked their way back east to the mountains in time for Rendezvous at Green River.

When the white intruders left, the news spread quickly among the Indian groups, and everyone was summoned to a Circle.

A spokesman began with, "White men have come to our land again. We watched them kill our beaver. We could not gather food when they were here. We are not safe when they come. We have to run and hide. It is not good. We must stop the white men from coming to our land."

Many groups loosely followed Cap John, and he spoke next. "We can do nothing to stop the white men from coming to our land. More and more will come. Our land will be covered with white men. We will run, but there will be no place left to hide."

The first spokesman responded with a question to the men in the Circle. "Tell us," he said, "what should we do with the white men?"

A young man shouted, "Kill them! We will get weapons from our cousins and kill all the white men that come!"

A burst of agreement went around the Circle. "Kill them! Kill them!"

Cap John held up his hand and silenced the voices. "They have more guns and horses than we will ever have. They will kill us."

"If they take away our food, we will starve," the young man answered. "Is it better to starve than be killed with a gun?"

"Not all white men kill," Cap John protested. "I spent time with them. They did not kill me."

"Then what should we do?" the spokesman asked desperately.

Cap John answered, "Show them we are friendly. Make them

our friends. The next time white men come, we will send a group to welcome them."

"Our bravest hunters?" the spokesman asked.

"No," said Cap John. "They might mistake them for warriors."

"Then should we send our old men and women?"

"No." Cap John shook his head. "They might feel we were being disrespectful."

"Our young boys?"

"Yes," Cap John agreed thoughtfully. "Our young boys would not be mistaken for warriors, and they would bring greetings with respect and honor."

So it was agreed around the Circle. The next group of white men who came to the Humboldt would be welcomed by the people's finest young boys.

CHAPTER 6
1833

===

FORT VANCOUVER

Nathaniel Wyeth had complete confidence in the skillful boat handlers as they navigated the swift, high waters of the Willamette River. He looked about with awe at the gently rising slopes covered with deep green fir trees. Fifty miles to the east, the snow-covered Mount Hood rose silhouetted against a cloudless blue sky.

Wyeth and his few remaining men had reached Fort Vancouver at the end of October. They had been fortunate in staying ahead of the winter snows over the Blue Mountains, but faced continual rain coming down the Columbia River.

They had gratefully accepted John McLoughlin's hospitality, which began with dry clothes, a warm fire, and a hot meal. After the meal, McLoughlin had invited Wyeth into the Bachelor's Hall while Wyeth's men were made comfortable in a barracks building.

When they were alone, McLoughlin related the news he had received. "Your ship, Mr. Wyeth, hit a reef along the coast of South America and sank."

Wyeth's first thought was for his men. He had encouraged them, time and again, to continue on by saying they would be rewarded once the salmon business was established.

"I can manage," he said to McLoughlin. "My concern is for my men."

McLoughlin understood and replied, "There is a ship leaving soon for the Sandwich Islands. From there they can get passage home. If they want to stay and work, I can give them employment. As for you, Mr. Wyeth, I offer hospitality for the winter."

For the next three months, the rainy weather persisted. The temperature remained mild by Bostonian standards, and the middle of February brought increasingly sunny days.

Surprisingly, the time had passed quickly for Wyeth. The available reading material was limited, but much information was gained from long conversations with McLoughlin and his stepson Tom McKay. A ship had put in from England bringing information from that part of the world, and monthly messengers came down the Columbia River carrying news from the circuit of Hudson Bay forts.

When McLoughlin and McKay invited him to boat up the Willamette River to the Falls, Wyeth accepted willingly, trying to keep his enthusiasm from building to flagrant excitement.

"We are looking for a suitable site for Tom and his family to settle on," McLoughlin explained.

Wyeth had learned during the winter that Tom McKay was the eldest child of McLoughlin's wife, Margaret. Margaret's father was a Swiss fur trader and her mother a Chippewa Indian of the Red River Country. Margaret had remained in Sault Ste. Marie with her three daughters when her first husband, Alexander McKay, went to the American Fort Astoria in 1810, taking thirteen-year-old Tom with him. McKay was killed, leaving Tom without family at Fort Astoria. After McKay's death, Margaret married McLoughlin, and fourteen years later, the family was reunited with Tom when McLoughlin was assigned to Fort Vancouver. By then Tom was married and the father of a son.

Tom was tall and well built, with light-brown hair and dark eyes. He was pleasant and companionable and loved to talk, often stretching the truth to make a better story. Wyeth had spent many hours with him through the winter, listening to tales of adventure shared by others who had passed through McLoughlin's Bachelor's Hall.

As the boat moved upstream, McKay broke the silence. "I plan to pick land on the south side of the Willamette, somewhere above the Falls. Or I might go north, somewhere around Wapato Island."

Wyeth nodded. During the winter conversations, he had become familiar with the story of how, three years earlier, a few released Hudson Bay trappers of French origins had decided to settle with their Indian wives and families up the river beyond the Falls, which offered abundant rich prairie farming land.

"When the men settled upriver," McLoughlin said, "I staked a company claim to the east shore of the Willamette River at the Falls. If the French Prairie settlement continues to grow, we'll build a gristmill there, so the men can deliver their grain without having to portage the Falls. The flour can then be sent on down for shipment."

Wyeth's enthusiasm could no longer be silenced. "The island that you speak of to the north—Wapato Island—neither of you have plans for it. I'll go back east. I'll get backers to dispatch another ship. In the fall, I'll come back and open my salmon cannery there!"

McLoughlin and McKay exchanged glances. Company orders were to discourage—and prevent if possible—any American business or settlement from forming in the dual-occupied territory.

Wyeth was too excited to notice that neither man answered him. "I will prepare to leave for the East immediately," he continued.

McLoughlin nodded once and said, "Godspeed."

GREEN RIVER

Capt. Bonneville watched from his fort with feelings of disgust as trappers, traders, and Indians gathered in the Green River Valley for Rendezvous.

His party had arrived at Pierre's Hole the previous year too late for the gathering. He had gotten a report of what had taken place from the handful of trappers still there and found out that the next year's meeting was scheduled for Green River.

He then proceeded on to Green River, picked a spot upstream that gave a clear view of the valley, and had his men construct a fort.

He and his party, under Joseph Walker's guidance, had then gone on to the Salmon and Snake Rivers. They found the Indians there helpful and friendly, but the rivers had been well trapped, and they had very few pelts with them when they returned to Green River in July. He had assumed the gathering would be at his fort, but trappers from the American Fur Company were camped about four miles away. Next to them, the Rocky Mountain Fur Company had set up camp. Farther up the valley were camps of Shoshone and Snake Indians.

Bonneville learned that during the winter, William Sublette and Robert Campbell, who had the previous year sold their holdings in the Rocky Mountain Company to Milton Sublette and John Fitzpatrick, had formed a new company called the Saint Louis Missouri Fur Company and were now challenging the American Fur Company backed by John Jacob Astor. William Sublette was not at Rendezvous but had taken materials by boat up the Missouri River and was building competition posts adjacent to American Fur Company posts.

Robert Campbell was bringing supplies to Rendezvous when he met Thomas Fitzpatrick, who negotiated purchase of the supplies and brought them on to Green River, arriving three days before the American Fur Company supplies arrived.

Bonneville observed, however, that even though the three rival companies were trying to out-trade, out-trap, and outwit each other, all parties were in good humor at the summer gathering.

Campbell had brought a variety of people with him, and Bonneville was delighted to entertain Sir William Drummond Stewart, wealthy Scotsman, and his entourage, who had made the trip west for pleasure. Nathaniel Wyeth also added an element to the gathering when he stopped on his way back to Boston.

Bonneville had made no profit with his trapping endeavors and found out little about the country. He now decided to send Joseph Walker on to California in the dual capacity of trapper and explorer while he and the rest of his men returned west and attempted to penetrate the Hudson Bay Company area along the Columbia River. He instructed Walker to recruit his own men for the trip to California and select his own route.

When Walker received his orders, he spent time with Milton Sublette, learning of the latter man's experiences, before deciding he would follow Sublette's route to the Humboldt and find his way south from there. He recruited forty men to accompany him and a few days later said farewell to Bonneville.

HUMBOLDT LAKE

It was October, and Joseph Walker and his party were nearing Humboldt Lake. After leaving Rendezvous, they had followed the Green River and the Bear River. There were buffalo in the area, and Walker had ordered every man to prepare no less than sixty pounds of jerky for his pack. Exactly what lay between them and California was unknown. Food might be plentiful, or it might be scarce. Walker believed in being prepared for the worst.

Suddenly two shots were heard. Walker wheeled his horse and headed back down the trail. He found one of his men dismounted with a rifle in his hands, looking at two dead, unarmed Indians who appeared to have been walking toward him.

"Why did you kill them?" Walker demanded.

"Why not?" the man answered.

Walker dismounted, grabbed the man by the neck with his left hand, and wrested the rifle from him with his right, saying, "From now on, you ride unarmed."

The man mounted his horse and followed Walker back to the head of the line, where Walker ordered a halt, informed his men what had happened, and told them that any more casual killing of Indians would be met with a like fate for the killer. Upset by the killing, he ordered an early stop for making camp.

Two young Paiute boys were on a familiar trail when one sensed something. He held up his hand and motioned his friend to proceed cautiously. They soon spotted, below them, a camp with many horses and many men wearing white man's clothing.

Undetected by Joseph Walker and his men, they sped back to their people to tell the news.

The following morning, Walker's group continued on. In the meantime, a signal had gone out for the young boys from all the bands up and down the area to come to the designated meeting place in the hills to prepare for the welcoming of the white men, as agreed upon at the Circle meeting.

The boys brought with them their finest skin breechcloths. Laughing and pretending not to be afraid, they covered their bodies with the brightest colored designs they knew: circles, half-moons, dots, wedges, triangles. With great excitement, they watched as the white men made camp.

After camp had been set up, Walker, as was his custom, brought out his spyglass to survey the country. This afternoon, his glass revealed more than countryside. It revealed hundreds of Indians who had gathered at a distance to watch the welcoming.

Walker put down his glass, turned to his assistant, and said, "They've come to avenge the killings our man made."

Immediately the order went out to secure the camp. A breastwork of the men's packs was thrown up, and the horses were brought inside it and tied to a picket line. Guns were poised.

At a signal from Cap John, the young men started down the hills, smiling, prancing, and high-stepping.

As the brightly painted boys came closer, Walker's men leveled their rifles. The unsuspecting boys lifted their prancing feet higher. The first round of gunshot reached their ears like a clap of thunder. The second round sent them scattering and falling to the ground. The third round sent them running for their lives. Thirty-nine were killed.

In the morning, Walker and his men cautiously broke camp and headed for the Sierras and California. When they were gone, the people, with great mourning, gathered their dead.

Cap John disappeared. He knew that now the people would seek weapons, and the next time white men came, they would fight.

CHAPTER 7
1834

OREGON TRAIL

Nathaniel Wyeth, heading west once again, could not put into words what floated across his mind, rippling through his thoughts like the wind through the rolling grass of the plains. His dream had become reality. But the dimensions of his dream had never been of this size. He had never envisioned the expanse of sky that exploded around him, or the brilliance of color that invaded his mind.

Returning to Boston the past November, he had been met by his friends, family, and investors with a mixture of awe, disbelief, resentment, and admiration. The money entrusted to him was gone, but as he talked enthusiastically about a second try, Henry Hall put up a sizable amount to back him. Others followed, and soon the Columbia River Fishing and Trading Company had been formed. To build the processing plant, he again chartered a ship to carry supplies around the Horn and up the Columbia River to Wapato Island. He planned to send a load of processed salmon back east on the same ship.

He had also, on his way back east the previous year, struck a deal with Milton Sublette and Thomas Fitzpatrick to bring supplies to the 1834 Rendezvous for the Rocky Mountain Fur Company. The contracted supplies were now in the caravan's lumbering wagons. Unfortunately, Milton had suffered a leg injury and was unable to make this trip. Before Wyeth left Massachusetts, however, a number of other people had approached him regarding riding west with him. Besides adventurers, he had taken on a small group of missionaries and naturalist Thomas Nuttall. The five missionaries, headed by Jason Lee, were going west in response to a request made by a group of Nez Perce and Flathead Indians who had made their way to Saint Louis seeking the white man's "book of heaven." They were backed by the American Missionary Society of the Methodist Episcopal Church. But, as the missionaries had no defined destination, Wyeth was not eager to have them join his train. In the end, he relented. He remembered that he, also, had traveled by faith on his first trip.

CALIFORNIA

It had taken Hall Kelley nearly two years to reach California. He spent time in New Orleans, which still retained the French sights and sounds of its origin, before heading west into the Texas territory of Mexico. There he found the American settlement teeming with emotion.

Mexico's Constitution of 1824 guaranteed the Texans separate statehood once the province was sufficiently developed. However, ever since Mexico had gained its independence from Spain in 1821, the government had been torn by conspiracy and confusion. Now it seemed General Santa Anna was the strongest leader in the country. President Jackson had offered to buy Texas from Mexico for $5 million and been turned down. Recently Sam Houston, personal friend of President Jackson and former congressman from Tennessee, had arrived, and word circulated that he had been sent by the president to gather intelligence about the conditions in the country.

When Kelley left Texas, he went up to Santa Fe and connected with trappers heading toward California. He found the trappers miserable traveling companions and decided almost immediately they were not the type of colonizing people he was looking for.

When they reached California and the trappers decided to travel north, Kelley decided to go south. He reached the mission-type hamlet of San Diego and had been there but a few hours when he heard of another American in the vicinity: one named Ewing Young, talking about Oregon.

Young had reached California two years earlier after leaving Taos and had connected with David Jackson and his men. Jackson had been successful in purchasing a herd of cattle, and when he and his drovers started east with the herd, Young had accompanied them until they reached the mountain pass. At that point he turned back to California and spent the summer and fall trapping sea otters, which he sold to ship merchants doing business in the San Francisco Bay area.

While in the San Francisco area, he again met a Hudson Bay party. Among them was John Turner, one of the members of Jedediah Smith's party who had escaped. Turner was glad to meet an American again, and when Young started south, Turner left the Hudson Bay party and joined him.

As Young and Turner traveled together, a plan formed. Young's finances were getting short, so they agreed to return to San Diego for the winter, and in the spring, Young would purchase as many horses as he could with his remaining money. With Turner as guide, they would drive the horses up through California to the Oregon Country, where Turner was sure they would find a lucrative market for the animals at French Prairie.

On their way to San Diego, they heard the news a messenger had brought from Mexico to all the missions: a new law had been made. "California now belongs to Mexico. All padres must leave the missions. The land belongs to Mexico."

When Hall Kelley located Young in San Diego, he introduced himself, saying, "I am Hall Kelley of Massachusetts, an agent of the Oregon Colonizing Company seeking recruits. I hear you are preparing to leave for Oregon."

"Soon as I round up a herd of horses," Young said.

"A herd of horses?"

"Farms are startin' in Oregon, and they need horses."

The news of farms in Oregon sounded encouraging to Kelley,

but he had no intention of waiting around for Young to round up a herd of horses. He'd made it this far alone. He'd push on, seeking colonizing recruits as he went.

GREEN RIVER RENDEZVOUS

Riders approached as Wyeth's caravan neared Green River. One of them called out, "What's in them wagons?"

"Rendezvous supplies," Wyeth called back.

The rider scratched his beard. "Supplies? Supplies are already here. William Sublette brought them three days ago."

With that announcement, everyone knew who had been in charge of the mysterious caravan that had passed them one evening in the dark of night and rushed on ahead. Milton Sublette's own brother had double-crossed them by bringing supplies to Rendezvous and making sure he got there first.

"But you said you had a contract to furnish supplies," Jason Lee said hopefully.

Wyeth was angry. "I did, but here in the wilds, with Milton not with me, there's nothing I can do about it. By now the men will have spent all their money, and I'm left with a caravan of worthless merchandise."

It was a subdued, unhappy group that made camp that night and tried to sleep in spite of the noise.

In the morning, Wyeth called the group together. An idea had come to him during the night. "I won't be defeated," he announced. "I'll tour the camp for a few days, sell what I can, and give you folks a chance to rest. Then we'll move out, find a likely place, and build a trading post."

FORT VANCOUVER

John McLoughlin waited daily for word from Peter Ogden. Ogden had been called to Fort Vancouver in the spring and given instructions to temporarily leave his post on the Nass River to oversee the building of a new trading fort on the Stikine River.

The site chosen for the fort was in British-controlled territory;

however, the mouth of the Stikine lay in Russian-controlled Alaska. Ogden's first assignment was to gain Russian permission for entry to the river. McLoughlin knew Russian-British relations were strained and that astute negotiating and persuasion would be required.

While waiting to hear whether Ogden had been successful, he received two other pieces of information. One was that Nathaniel Wyeth was on his way back to establish his salmon business on Wapato Island. McLoughlin had hoped when he bid Wyeth farewell the previous year that Wyeth would be content, once he reached the east, to remain there.

The pressing matter at the moment, however, was the portion of the report that stated Wyeth was building a trading post on the Snake River. This, of course, was completely contrary to Hudson Bay Company policy, which stated that all American activities in the area should be discouraged. McLoughlin immediately sent word to Tom McKay to reroute his field brigade and take whatever action he deemed necessary to stop or counter the building of the post.

The other news, carried by ship from the governor of California, warned that horse thieves were heading north from California with a large herd of stolen horses. McLoughlin would not tolerate thievery. He made ready to dispatch a brigade from the fort to head south for purposes of checking out this report.

OREGON TRAIL

After leaving Green River, Wyeth had taken the caravan on up the Snake River. Nine miles above the mouth of the Portneuf River, all able hands were put to work building the post. A fort, constructed of logs, was surrounded by a fifteen-foot wall made of cottonwood trees set on end. The enclosure was eighty feet square with two eight-square-foot bastions at opposite angles. The portholes in the bastions were large enough for guns only. Quarters for the men who would remain to staff the fort were made of hewed logs covered with mud brick. Square holes were left in the roof for windows. When the fort was completed and the goods stored, Wyeth ran up an American flag made of sheeting, red flannel, and blue swatches and christened the post Fort Hall in honor of Henry Hall, his main Boston backer.

Once again on the trail, he pushed the group as rapidly as possible. He knew snow came early to the Blue Mountains. Stopping to build Fort Hall had taken away precious travel time.

Two days after leaving Fort Hall, Wyeth and his men met Tom McKay and his brigade of Indians and French Canadians. Wyeth, unaware of McKay's mission, welcomed him warmly. The two parties camped together that night. After the evening meal, Wyeth and McKay sat apart from the rest of the company. By a flickering campfire, with strains of fiddle music in the background, Wyeth told McKay what scoundrels the American trappers were and how poorly they had treated him.

McKay agreed and complimented Wyeth on his ingenuity in building a fort and trading post along the main route to the West and hospitably released members of his party to travel as escorts with Wyeth's group to Fort Vancouver. McKay promised to join them as soon as his business was taken care of.

After Wyeth and his caravan left in the morning and were out of sight, McKay set about building Fort Boise, a British trading post on the Snake River that would rival the American Fort Hall.

French Prairie

Jason Lee was a large, friendly, thirty-one-year-old man. Born in Quebec to New England parents, he had received his education at Wesleyan Academy in Wilbraham, Massachusetts, and had become licensed to preach in 1830. When he heard the call for missionaries to go into the Oregon Country, he volunteered, along with his nephew Daniel, Cyrus Shepherd, Philip Edwards, and Mr. Ewen. They were accepted by the society, booked passage with Wyeth, and headed west.

Thanks to the leadership of Wyeth and the escort provided by Tom McKay, they crossed the Blue Mountains safely, boated down the Columbia River, and received a warm welcome at Fort Vancouver from Dr. McLoughlin. McLoughlin invited them to hold services at the fort, provided an escort for them, and encouraged them to explore the Willamette Valley.

At French Prairie, they visited the community of the retired Hudson Bay trappers and their families. The soil at French Prairie was good for farming, and the weather was fine, but Lee was instantly aware of the main reason the men had settled there rather than going home: their wives and children would not be welcome in an all-white society.

Although this was not the group that had requested the white man's "book of heaven," Lee saw a need for Christian guidance, children who needed education, and an area that would allow for farming in connection with his group's mission work. Lee and his group selected a location in close proximity to French Prairie, sixty miles up from Fort Vancouver, and began construction on a small but permanent settlement.

OREGON COUNTRY

Ewing Young, John Turner, and a few drovers left San Jose in August with ninety-eight head of horses and mules. They found Hall Kelley waiting for them when they reached San Francisco. Kelley, having heard reports of renegade Indians between him and the Columbia River and having been unsuccessful in his search for recruits, had decided to wait and go on with Young. A few days after leaving San Francisco, they overtook another party resting their herd of horses. There were signs the horses had been driven hard and needed the rest.

Young asked the man in charge no questions other than, "You headin' for the Columbia?"

"No," the man replied. "We're aiming to swing east before we get that far and head for the Plains. We'd like to ride with you, though, till we get through the hostile Indian country ahead."

Young agreed. There was safety in numbers. His biggest concern at that point was with Hall Kelley, who had complained of feeling sick the first morning out and continued to grow worse. The day the other group left them to go east, Kelley could scarcely stay in his saddle. He made it through the night and only with the greatest determination mounted his horse the next morning.

They were scarcely under way when one of the drovers yodeled, "Horsemen approaching!"

Recognizing the British flag they carried, Young galloped on ahead of the herd, reined in his horse, and awaited the approach of the brigade leader. The leader, eyeing Young suspiciously, identified his unit as being from the Hudson Bay Company, headquartered at Fort Vancouver.

"A ship from California put in to the Columbia recently, and the captain reported a herd of stolen horses had left California heading this way. Know anything about it?"

"Nope," Young replied.

"Do you have a document of sale for your herd?"

"Nope. Do business with a handshake."

"Seen any other herds coming this way?"

"None that looked stolen," Young replied.

"Mind if we take a look at what you have?"

"Go ahead. Nothin' wrong with my horses. Got a man who's mighty sick."

"What is he sick with?"

"Don't know."

The brigade moved around and through the herd. When the brigade leader found Kelley, he spoke briefly with him and returned to Young.

"With your permission," he said, "we'll take Mr. Kelley directly to Fort Vancouver for medical attention."

Young agreed. He was glad to be rid of the responsibility of a man as sick as Kelley.

The brigade returned, at a fast pace, to Fort Vancouver and delivered Kelley to the company hospital, where he was diagnosed as having malaria.

Two days later, Young and his party were met by a messenger from the fort asking to meet with Ewing Young.

"Dr. McLoughlin sends this message," he reported. "Do not attempt to buy supplies at the fort. Dr. McLoughlin does not do business with a horse thief."

"Horse thief?" Young said in unbelief. "Horse thief? Me?"

The messenger, having delivered his message, turned and sped away.

Young poured out his feelings of anger to Turner, who listened but could only answer that this was McLoughlin's territory, and McLoughlin's word was law.

Once Young realized he had no recourse, he stopped short of the Willamette River, where tree-covered hills rolled off into the distance. He found a spot of level land with lush, green grass, set up camp, and staked out a land claim.

CHAPTER 8
1835

===

FORT VANCOUVER

Wyeth was taking a short break from work on the construction of Fort William on Wapato Island. He had walked closer to the water's edge to observe the myriad of birds that had descended on the river when he saw a boat approaching. It was a man from Fort Vancouver with a message from Hall Kelley.

The message had been written by Kelley on a small piece of parch paper sealed with wax. "Come at once. Urgent."

Wyeth took time only to inform his men he was leaving before boarding the boat to be rowed to the fort. He had visited Kelley at the company hospital upon his arrival in the fall and had found a very sick and bitter man.

After listening to Kelley's verbal attacks on the British, on Fort Vancouver, and especially on John McLoughlin, Wyeth had remarked, "There could be some merit to your feelings for the British and perhaps Fort Vancouver, but I find it somewhat contrary that you should harbor thoughts of hatred and mistrust for a man who has saved your life."

This had brought such an outburst of venomous remarks that Wyeth took his departure as quickly as possible and on future visits refrained from any like comments. When Kelley was well enough to leave the hospital, McLoughlin had housed him in a barracks room under guarded supervision. Wyeth found him there.

Kelley greeted him with, "McLoughlin is shipping me out tomorrow."

"Shipping you out?"

"He says there's a company ship leaving for the Sandwich Islands in the morning. He's putting me on it, along with a man from up the valley. He's given him seven pounds to book passage for me on the first ship leaving the islands for America."

That sounded very generous to Wyeth, but he replied, "I'm certain the man he has chosen to accompany you is honest, and you can trust him to arrange good passage for you." He continued the conversation with news of Ewing Young. Young was developing quite a spread a few miles back from the river in the Chehalem Valley. He had survived, in spite of McLoughlin's refusal to do business with him, by bartering his horse and mule herds with the French Prairie settlement for needed supplies.

Kelley did not respond to Wyeth's comment, and soon there came a knock at the door. Wyeth opened the door and was surprised to see one of the men who had come west with him and gone on up the valley with Jason Lee.

"I'm here to make arrangements with Mr. Kelley for our trip tomorrow," he said.

Wyeth cordially welcomed him into the room, and when the moment was right, inquired as to the state of Jason Lee and the mission.

"The winter went well," the man replied. "We erected buildings for both school and church. School is in session, and the children are very apt scholars. I was able to help Pastor Lee some with their training. I was sorry to leave, but when McLoughlin offered me passage for accompanying Mr. Kelley back to the States, I acknowledged that my adventure was over."

Wyeth bid them farewell, knowing Kelley was in good hands.

GREEN RIVER RENDEZVOUS

Capt. Bonneville stopped at Green River on his way east. He

was returning home to he knew not what. He had overstayed his authorized leave from the Army by more than a year. His fur business had failed. He had penetrated the Hudson Bay Company territory all the way to the Columbia River, gathering what little information he could of their outposts. At Fort Walla Walla, he had reverted to establishing friendly relations with the Flathead and Nez Perce people and had spent a pleasant winter in their company.

While living with the Nez Perce, he met two of their members who had gone with two members of the Flathead Tribe to Saint Louis four years earlier, seeking men who would come to their people and teach them the black book. They were told their request would be sent on east, and they returned to their tribes and were disappointed that no one had come.

A few days after Bonneville's arrival in Green River, the supply train arrived. With the train were two men sent by the American Board of Commissioners of Foreign Missions. Bonneville was pleased to meet them and hear that the board had received the request made by the Indian delegation to Saint Louis. Dr. Marcus Whitman and Rev. Samuel Parker had volunteered to make the trip west. When the two men heard there were forty Flathead and Nez Perce lodges in the valley, they arranged to contact their leaders.

When Bonneville saw them again, they reported that the reception they had received from the Indians led them to believe they had found a promising field for missionary work. Their plan was for Whitman to return east immediately and seek permission from the board to establish a mission in Oregon Country and ask that additional associates be sent out. Parker would continue on with a group of trappers to Pierre's Hole and from there find Indian guidance to the Columbia, where he would locate a suitable site for the mission. The two men had agreed to meet again at the next Rendezvous.

Capt. Bonneville extended an invitation to Dr. Whitman to accompany his wagon train east. Dr. Whitman accepted, saying he was eager to receive as much information as he could about the area and the people he hoped to minister to.

CHAPTER 9
1836

===

CALIFORNIA

On May 8, 1836, on the San Diego beach in Spanish California, the brig *Alert* prepared to sail for home. The ship, loaded deep with its cargo of furs, had lost several of its crew members. Among those remaining was a young man from Boston, Richard Dana. Dana had been a seaman long enough to know that in two months, they would be sailing off Cape Horn, where July was not summer but the worst winter month. They would be traveling in high seas, facing snow and gales and nights eighteen hours long.

"Never mind," shouted Dana. "We're homeward bound!"

A passenger, also homeward bound, had spoken with the second mate, who related to Dana, "I can't remember the man's name, but he says he knows you. He has white hair and has spent his time here wandering the beach, picking up such truck as flowers and shells. Must be crazy rich to amuse himself that way. In fact, here he comes now."

Dana spotted the man. He was barefoot with his trousers rolled up to his knees, wearing a sailor's peajacket and a wide straw hat.

Dana knew him at once. "Why, that's Professor Nuttall, my botany instructor at Harvard College!"

Dana, born to a prominent family in Cambridge, Massachusetts, had been in his junior year at Harvard when a case of measles affected his eyesight and caused him to drop out of school. Having an adventurous nature, he signed on as a common seaman on a brig scheduled to sail around Cape Horn to California with an assorted cargo of foodstuffs, hardware, clothing, jewelry, furniture, and fireworks. They were taking back furs and hides.

Thomas Nuttall, from England, had a passion for botany. He had accompanied John Jacob Astor's party in 1811 and left them to travel with Manuel Lisa's party. He returned to England during the War of 1812 but later came back to America and in 1823 accepted a position at Harvard. In 1834, the same year Dana withdrew, Nuttall quit Harvard to accompany Nathaniel Wyeth on his trip west. After reaching Fort Vancouver, he sailed to Hawaii (Sandwich Islands) and from there to California to book passage back east.

Dana and Nuttall exchanged greetings, but Dana had no time to talk; the ship's crew was shorthanded. Nuttall went below to his passenger's quarters.

Washington, DC

President Jackson reread Capt. Bonneville's report of his trapping expedition. Since he had overstayed his Army leave and sent no word to anyone during the entire time he was gone, the Army had assumed him dead and dropped him from their rolls. In his report, he explained that circumstances had prevented him from corresponding. He also explained that he had failed to bring in enough furs to offset expenses, because his concentration had been spent on penetrating British territory. This had been accomplished at Powder River, near the Malheur, where he reported there were few natural resources and no British in sight, with the land peopled by diggers who wanted mirrors.

Twice he had been to British Fort Walla Walla on the Columbia, where he had not been genially received. He had attended annual Rendezvous and spent much time with the friendly Nez Perce and Flathead Indians. He had once been forced to join in a fight against the Blackfeet Indians—who were, he reported, "Ishmaelites of the first degree."

He had severed connections with his guide, Joseph Walker, who had married a Shoshone woman and chosen to make his home in the wilds of the West.

Jackson smiled and laid aside Bonneville's report. He knew which people to contact and would soon have Bonneville reinstated in the Army.

The second report the president studied was from Sam Houston. Texans had gained their independence from Mexico. They were defeated at the Alamo in March, but in April Houston had captured Santa Anna at San Jacinto and forced him to sign treaties agreeing to withdraw his Mexican troops and recognize the Rio Grande as the southwestern boundary of Texas.

Jackson pondered what to do about Texas. He would like to recognize the independent republic, but timing was bad. If he recognized a slavery republic, he would lose the support from the northern states that he needed to assure the election of his successor, Martin Van Buren. He would, he decided, hold off recognizing Texas until after the election. He knew he could count on his friend Sam Houston to hold things together until then.

Once again he picked up Bonneville's report. He needed more and better information, he decided, than what Bonneville had given him. He called for his assistant and told him to bring William Slacum to him as quickly as possible.

Slacum was a sharp young Navy lieutenant. He was intelligent and trustworthy, and Jackson was now ready to act on a plan they had discussed. He would send Slacum, by private ship, around the Horn to the Columbia, where he would pose, for the benefit of the British, as a private gentleman whose only interest was to see the country.

GREEN RIVER RENDEZVOUS

There were white women in camp. Dr. Whitman had presented his request to the board successfully. He had returned west to build a mission and brought with him his bride, Narcissa. Rev. and

Mrs. Henry Spalding had come with them, along with one other associate, William Gray.

Whitman had arranged, once again, for travel with the supply train, this year under the direction of Thomas Fitzpatrick. The Whitmans and the Spaldings each had their own wagon.

The ladies were greeted at Rendezvous with awe and respect. A cavalcade parade of six hundred Indians, dressed in their best, greeted them.

Nathaniel Wyeth had arrived at the camp a few days earlier to await their arrival. Wyeth was going home, this time for good. His ship had been struck by lightning and failed to make it in time for the salmon run. That left him without operating funds. He sold his building on Wapato Island to the Hudson Bay Company and also sold them Fort Hall. Then, accompanied by Thomas McKay, he headed for Rendezvous with a message from Rev. Parker for Dr. Whitman.

Rev. Parker had spent several pleasant months at Fort Vancouver and in the spring booked passage on a ship for New York. Dr. Whitman was deeply disappointed when he received Parker's message stating he had not located a mission site. The Whitmans and the Spaldings had come west relying on the promise that Parker would meet them at Rendezvous and take them to a definite site.

Wyeth discussed the problem with McKay, and McKay offered to escort the two couples to Fort Vancouver, where Mrs. Spalding, in frail health, could receive treatment. McKay told them their wagons would have to, unfortunately, be left behind. The trail to the Columbia would not accommodate wagons.

Wyeth felt a twinge of satisfactory revenge leaving Rendezvous for the last time. He had heard the word going around that, in fashionable circles, silk hats were becoming more popular than beaver hats.

FORT VANCOUVER

The fort had been abuzz with constant activity all fall. Peter Ogden had left in September from his annual summer trip to the fort to return to his family at his post at Fort Saint James on Stuart Lake. He had been commissioned chief factor in charge of the New Caledonia District, which covered a huge area to the north that contained eight company forts and five tribes of Indians. Ogden had been unsuccessful in his negotiations with the Russians over access to the Stikine River in Alaska, but McLoughlin had been released from further activity in the matter, as it was now being resolved in diplomatic channels between London and Russia.

Immediately after Ogden left, a company ship arrived from the Sandwich Islands bringing Rev. Herbert Beaver, a clergyman of the Church of England, and his wife, Jane. Six years earlier, McLoughlin had requested a missionary be sent to the fort from England. During the six-year wait for his request to be filled, he had conducted services himself every Sunday. McLoughlin would have preferred a Roman Catholic priest but considered a Church of England clergyman acceptable. He envisioned a man like Jason Lee, who would work with the Indians, teaching them not only religion but how to till the land, raise food, and adjust their lifestyle.

His hopes faded when he met the ship and watched as Pastor Beaver and his wife debarked. Beaver was a short man with a high-pitched voice and a smug face. His wife, Jane, tossed her chin in the air as she looked about her. Pointing to an Indian village in the distance, she asked, "Are those pigsties?"

It took all of McLoughlin's self-control to remain calm when Beaver made his next remark, pointing to Mrs. McLoughlin and Mrs. Douglas, who were standing a few feet away.

"Let those two gaudy creatures out before my wife and I approach."

McLoughlin had them settled, complaining, in a house as quickly as he could. Before the week was out, Tom McKay arrived at the fort with the Whitmans and the Spaldings.

Eliza Spalding was given bed rest. Twenty-eight-year-old Narcissa Whitman, a charming, friendly, talented woman, was the daughter of Judge Prentiss of New York and had been a teacher whose life's desire was to go to the mission field. She and Dr. Whitman had married the preceding February and immediately started on their pilgrimage west.

Whitman and Spalding rested a few days, and then, leaving the women at the fort, left to locate mission sites. As he had with Jason Lee, McLoughlin pointed out the dangers of locating missions in the Upper Columbia area and encouraged them to locate in the valley. The men assured him they had been called by the Nez Perce, and they would be safe.

Early in December, they returned for their wives, who had become fond friends with Mrs. McLoughlin and the other women at the fort.

Whitman had located a site a few miles east of Fort Walla Walla, and Spalding's site was at Lapwai on the Clearwater River.

"The Lord directed us," Spalding declared. "The Nez Perce are much rejoiced that we have come."

When Dr. McLoughlin heard their supplies were nearly exhausted, he replenished their goods from his stores, asking in return only that they agree not to employ men at higher wages than what he paid his men.

Scarcely had they bade farewell to the missionaries than a private ship arrived carrying a Mr. William Slacum, gentleman from the east, just stopping by for a visit.

CHAPTER 10
1837

OREGON COUNTRY

The day was warm for January, the sunshine bright, and William Slacum relaxed in the canoe heading upriver to visit Jason Lee.

Slacum had spent a pleasant two weeks at the fort, playing the part of the gentleman, partaking in the feasting and dancing and merriment of the holiday season, while collecting as much information as possible.

He heard stories of Peter Ogden. He heard how he had just missed meeting the Whitmans and the Spaldings. He heard how Nathaniel Wyeth had been treated better by the British than he had by the Americans and had retaliated by selling Forts William and Hall to the Hudson Bay Company. He heard how Hall Kelley, writer of bitter attacks against the British, had been sent back to Boston, and he heard the story of Ewing Young.

The previous spring, Ewing Young had attempted to expand his business by starting construction on a sawmill. When Wyeth sold Fort William, Young purchased a cauldron from him. Wyeth had planned to use the cauldron for pickling salmon; Young planned to use it as a distillery.

McLoughlin, knowing the demeaning affect alcohol had on the

native population, had forbidden supplying or serving it to them. He was at a loss to know how to handle the situation with Young.

As Slacum listened to the story, he saw the situation as an opportunity to strengthen American holdings in Oregon.

"If there were some way I could talk with Young, perhaps I could reason with him," he told McLoughlin.

McLoughlin suggested Jason Lee as the best person to arrange a meeting and ordered passage for Slacum to the mission.

When Slacum reached the mission, he was warmly greeted by Jason Lee. All was going well, Lee informed him. He was looking forward to the addition of two women to their staff. The women, mature teachers with a calling to be missionaries, had left Boston by ship and were wintering at Honolulu in the Sandwich Islands and would continue on to the mission in the spring.

Lee did have one concern, and it was the same as McLoughin's: he knew of Young's plans to build a brewery and to sell alcohol to whoever had the means to buy.

When Slacum asked for an escort to visit Young, saying he could possibly dissuade the brewery plans, Lee agreed to accompany him.

The following day, upon meeting Young, Slacum quickly got to the reason of their visit.

"I hear you have plans for a brewery," he said.

Young assured him that he had and took them to the cauldron of fermenting alcohol.

"Why are you doing this?" Slacum asked.

"Survival," Young answered. "McLoughlin refuses to deal with me. I've traded as much of my herd as I can."

Slacum asked, "Ever thought of bringing in more stock?"

"Nope. Takes money."

"I have a plan," Slacum said. "Get rid of the alcohol, and I'll help you raise money to form a cattle company. We'll ask the settlers in French Prairie to back you. When you have enough money, I'll give you free passage to California on my ship. You've brought a herd up once. You can do it again."

Young considered only a moment. He had wanted to get back

to California to secure papers that would clear his name as a horse thief. He extended his hand. Slacum grasped it.

As the fermenting alcohol bubbled out on the ground, Lee smiled. "Let me be your first investor," he said.

Back at the mission, they arranged for a meeting with the men from French Prairie. The plan was greeted with enthusiasm, and when the men heard both Lee and Slacum were investing in the company, they unanimously agreed to do likewise.

Slacum returned to Fort Vancouver and told McLoughlin what had taken place. McLoughlin, although becoming suspicious that Slacum was more than a private gentleman visitor, rethought his accusation of Ewing Young. If Young was willing to return to California, McLoughlin must have judged him wrongly.

"I believe I owe Ewing Young an apology," McLoughlin said. "And, if it's agreeable with him, I will invest in his cattle company."

Slacum carried the message back to Young, who accepted the apology, and the two set January 18 as the day they would sail for California.

French Prairie

The young Indian girls sat together on the lawn at the mission. As soon as the weddings were over, they would carry the food from the kitchen to the tables set up under the trees.

Things had happened so fast the last two months, the girls could hardly believe it. In May, Pastor Lee had informed them he was going to Fort Vancouver to bring back lady teachers who had come by ship from the East. Whispers went through the group. "Are they white ladies? What will they look like? How will they dress?"

A week later, the ladies arrived on horseback, escorted by Pastor Lee and Tom McKay. The trip from the fort to the mission had taken three days. They had boated from Fort Vancouver to the falls of the Willamette River, where McKay had met them with horses for the remainder of the trip.

Everyone in the settlement had gathered at the mission to meet them. The white ladies wore hats tied under their chins and dresses of calico with voluminous skirts.

"I would like a dress like that," one young girl whispered to another.

The ladies were named Anna Marie and Susan. The very next day, the women went to work on the rough log house called the mission. The house had two rooms, plus a kitchen and a schoolroom. In no time it was transformed from its drab interior to bright, cheerful living quarters.

The girls liked to be with Anna Marie. She was different. They wondered why her white face turned red whenever Pastor Lee talked to her. Then one day, very soon after they arrived, one of the girls overhead Anna Marie and Susan talking to each other.

Anna Marie said, "Jason asked me to marry him."

Susan gasped and said, "Cyrus Shepherd made the same request of me!"

The ladies seemed very happy. The young girl thought, *So that is how white people arrange marriage. That is strange. I would rather have Grandmother help me.*

Soon the announcement was made that Sunday, July 16, would be the wedding day for three couples. Charles Roe, an American settler, and Miss Nancy, a Callopooya Indian, were also getting married. The girls were pleased when Anna Marie asked them to help with the tables.

The weather for the wedding day was beautiful. When the girls saw the dress Anna Marie was wearing, they told her it was beautiful, too.

Anna Marie laughed and said, "I did not come west expecting to be married, so I brought no bridal dress with me. This one will have to do."

The wedding ceremony began with Jason Lee addressing the congregation gathered on the grass and seated among the trees. He stood in front of the people and said, "I have talked to you before of the importance of a church-blessed marriage. Now I will practice what I preach."

Then he walked to Anna Marie and held her hand while Pastor Daniel Lee spoke the words of marriage to them.

Anna Marie then stepped aside while her new husband spoke the marriage words to Cyrus and Susan and to Mr. Roe and Miss Nancy.

After all the couples were married, Jason Lee led the singing of hymns, offered prayers, and preached a sermon. After that his nephew Daniel Lee presided at the Communion of the Last Supper. People were encouraged to give testimonies for the Lord, and when that was over, they sang another hymn, and Jason said a closing prayer.

By now everyone was very hungry. The food was ready. The girls hastened to carry it to the tables.

It was October when Ewing Young rode slowly through the cheering, friendly crowd gathered again at the mission. He noticed a change. There was a homier atmosphere now that Jason and Anna Marie and Cyrus and Susan were married.

Nine months had passed since the organization of the Willamette Cattle Company and the raising of $1,600 to purchase cattle in California. On January 18, as planned, Young had boarded Slacum's ship at Fort Vancouver, along with his co-leader, Philip Edwards from the mission.

Slacum dropped them off in California on his way back to the East Coast. It took Young a few months to "take care of some personal business," as he put it. Along with taking care of his personal business, he had succeeded in gaining permission to drive seven hundred cattle out of California, provided they were purchased from the Mexican government.

It was July before the drovers, with much hallooing and growling and swearing, drove the cattle across the San Joaquin River. They rested for several days once they were across the river before starting north through the searing summer heat of the Sacramento Valley. A month later, they were ascending the slopes of the Siskiyou Mountains. Dust covered the faces of the men and filled their lungs as they struggled up the hot slopes. The cattle were hungry and weary.

Finally, toward the end of August, they came to a spot with plenty of grass and water where they could rest the cattle. Young allowed his men to kill one, and everyone feasted on beef.

As they started up the Siskiyou Pass, Young gave the word to be alert for Indian attacks. Malaria, he knew, had killed many Indians, and those remaining were fighters.

He was not wrong in his prediction. Indians were spotted off in the distance, out of gunshot range. Occasionally an arrow would zing out, its sender safely concealed in the brush. Several cattle were wounded, one so severely it was killed for food.

They pushed the herd on as rapidly as possible until they reached the tall, green grass of the Willamette Valley. It was early October when they approached French Prairie.

They left the herd grazing and rode on to the mission, where the settlers had gathered to welcome them. Once the cattle were delivered to their owners, Young would be released to return to his own holdings.

At the mission, he conversed with Jason Lee. Anna Marie was expecting a child, and Young was surprised when Jason told him he planned to leave for the East in the spring.

"Anna Marie is in good health and in good care," he said. "We need more supplies and recruits to accomplish the work to be done here. We've agreed it's time for me to go back and make our needs known to the board."

CHAPTER 11
1838

WASHINGTON, DC

John Quincy Adams rode in his carriage down the muddy streets of the city. For the last seven years, he had served in the House of Representatives, opposing President Jackson on all domestic issues and supporting only his foreign policy. He had watched Martin Van Buren win, with Jackson's support, the 1836 election and take office a year before.

The first railroad into Washington brought visitors from New York City and Philadelphia for Van Buren's inauguration. Adams felt a sense of satisfaction over the railroad, for it was an offshoot of his program of national improvements.

"They should also use the program to improve these muddy streets," he muttered.

He was not at all fond of Van Buren, but he had compassion for him. Van Buren had inherited tremendous problems. Two months after he took office, the economy of the country crashed. Adams had seen it building all during Jackson's administration.

For one thing, sales of public lands had not been limited to settlers. Land speculation was fueled when state banks and branches of the Bank of the United States made loans without security in gold and silver. Too late, Jackson attempted to limit land sales by requiring the government to accept only gold and silver in payment for public lands. This ended the speculation, but when banks could no longer make loans without security, they were forced to close, and the first great depression since the country had been founded began.

Other problems had to be dealt with: the slavery issue, removal of Indians to reservations, masses of unemployed people, boundary disputes.

Adams believed more than ever that the powers of government must be used for the benefit of all the people, not just for the benefit of those who clamored the loudest. He shook his head, thinking how unfair it was that Jackson had returned with honor to the Hermitage in Tennessee while his predecessor was dubbed "Martin Van Ruin."

FORT VANCOUVER

James Douglas, thirty-five years of age, tall, slim, and erect, descendant of Douglas, Earl of Angus, displayed the traits of his Scottish nobility ancestry with his dark skin, eyes, and hair.

Douglas stood calmly on the porch of the McLoughlin house and surveyed the fort. "It's mine," he told himself. "John is on his way to London, and I'm in charge."

Douglas had met McLoughlin nineteen years earlier, when he had arrived at Fort William as a new recruit of the Northwest Fur Company. McLoughlin was chief trader at the fort. They had immediately formed a friendship, and McLoughlin had personally taught him the fur trade. After the two companies merged, Douglas served his apprenticeship with the Hudson Bay Company at various posts before being assigned to Fort Vancouver as McLoughlin's assistant.

He had brought his wife of two years, Amelia Connally, with him. Their marriage had been performed according to the fur-trade customs. When Rev. Beaver arrived from England, Douglas arranged for him to remarry them according to the rites of the Church of England. This had caused a problem over McLoughlin's marriage. Rev. Beaver claimed McLoughlin was living in sin, since he and Margaret had not been married according to the church. Rev. Beaver offered to perform the rites for him. McLoughlin refused but did allow Douglas to remarry them in his capacity as justice of the peace. This was only one of many events that increased tension between Beaver and McLoughlin.

The eruption had occurred recently when McLoughlin, unable to control his temper any longer, raised his cane and soundly beat Beaver upon his shoulders. The following day, at an auction sale held in the public square, McLoughlin humbly apologized to Rev. Beaver for the indignity he had laid upon him the day before.

Rev. Beaver did not accept Mcloughlin's apology.

Douglas was now making arrangements for departure back to England for Beaver and his wife. He was also assisting Jason Lee with his plans for returning east. One more task McLoughlin had entrusted him with was welcoming two long-awaited priests from the Catholic Church. They had received a letter from the archbishop of Quebec that Abbes Blanchet and Demers were being dispatched to Fort Vancouver to establish a mission in the area.

WIND RIVER RENDEZVOUS

Jason Lee rode through the valley of the Wind River. It had been a hot July day, and the cool of the evening was refreshing. He had arrived safely with the British and soon would make his way east with Americans.

A week before he was scheduled to leave with the brigade from Fort Vancouver, he had conferred with James Douglas. Douglas reconfirmed the departure date of the brigade and that Tom McKay would meet them at Fort Hall. From Fort Hall, they would go on to Rendezvous, where the brigade was to meet and escort back several missionaries who were on their way to the Whitman Mission.

When they reached Fort Hall, they found it thriving under British control. The British were paying more for furs and charging less for supplies than the Americans were at Rendezvous, but the lure of alcohol, carousing, gambling, and horse racing still drew men to Rendezvous.

The Hudson Bay brigade spent a few days at Fort Hall before

leaving for Green River. They reached Green River in good time and were amazed to find no one there. A herd of buffalo grazed in the valley. This was the site of the deserted Fort Bonneville. Scrawled in charcoal on the door of a sagging building were the words, "Come to Popo Agie, Wind River."

The message was not signed, and everyone suspected the meeting site had been changed to discourage the British from attending. The Fort Vancouver brigade was not put off that easily and agreed they would follow the message. The next morning, they left for Popo Agie.

They found the encampment in a valley at the forks of the Popo Agie and Wind Rivers. The weather at midday was stifling hot, and the shade of the cottonwood trees was a welcome sight.

The American supply train, headed by Andrew Drips and an assistant, August Johann Sutter, had arrived, bringing with them the five missionaries and their wives. Sir William Drummond Stewart of Scotland had again accompanied the supply train for pleasure, plus another seventy or so men.

August Sutter, due to financial problems, had left his family in Switzerland four years earlier and gone to New York. In New York he had been successful in persuading investors to advance him capital, which he used to return a good profit on the Sante Fe Trail.

Stopping in Taos, he had met a French-Canadian trapper who told glowing tales of the perpetual summers in Spanish California. He had explained that when the California missions were broken up, the Mexican government gave or sold a few large estates to private Mexican landowners. They now forbade foreigners to own land without approval by the government and were especially intent on keeping Americans out. However, there were ways that the regulations could be avoided.

Sutter had listened with interest and decided that this was where he wanted to go. He arranged to accompany the American Fur Company to Rendezvous. From there he planned to go to Fort Vancouver and arrange passage to the Sandwich Islands. He had a plan for California!

Kit Carson and his men were in the valley, along with Joseph

Walker and his company of more than a hundred men and women and numerous children. Lee was glad they had not arrived on the Fourth of July; he had heard the stories going around of that drinking, riotous day. The missionaries reported they had been treated kindly by all in the camp, but not more than ten or twelve men had come to the outdoor worship services they gave on the Sabbath.

Present throughout the camp was an underlying feeling that the trapping business was about over. No one spoke directly about it, but Lee felt a sense of dissatisfaction among the men, hints that the trade was no longer profitable, and a sentiment the Americans could not compete with the resources of the Hudson Bay Company.

Riding through the valley, Lee wondered where next year's Rendezvous would be, if there was one. Who would be there? Where would he be? He rode on thinking of Anna Marie and the mission and the coming birth of his child.

BOSTON

Nathaniel Wyeth reached Boston safely after 1836 Rendezvous. He had spent $20,000 and failed to open Oregon to American business. Fortunately for him, he was able to resume his employment with Frederic Tudor Ice Company at three times his former salary and was now developing improved machinery for cutting and storing ice.

The "Alert" also returned safely to Boston harbor, and Richard Dana was back at Harvard College, working toward his law degree and writing a book about his sea travels.

MISSOURI RIVER

Jason Lee had traveled steadily since leaving Wind River and was taking a welcome rest at the Shawnee Mission on the Missouri River when a runner arrived with a packet of letters for him.

He opened the packet and found letters of sympathy, along with a letter from James Douglas informing him Anna Marie had died on June 26, two days after the death of their newborn baby boy. Douglas had arranged for a relay of runners to overtake Lee with the message.

Grief-stricken, Lee could only repeat, "They are in heaven. They are in heaven."

Nez Perce Country

Joe Meek had lingered on at Rendezvous and was among the last of the trappers to leave. No definite plans had been made for the next year. Andrew Drips, not knowing whether a supply train would be dispatched the next season, decided to stay on in the mountains for the winter.

Twenty-eight-year-old Meek was no puritan. While a teenager, he'd left his Virginia home without the blessing of his English-heritage family, headed west to Missouri, and joined William Sublette's Rendezvous supply train of 1829. For the next nine years, he traveled the West with William and Milton Sublette, Jedediah Smith, Joseph Walker, Jim Bridger, and Kit Carson. At times he traveled alone. He had his share of narrow escapes, but never missed a Rendezvous.

With him when he left Wind River were his old friends and neighbors Robert Newell and Caleb Wilkins. They went to the Salmon River, found trapping scarce, and continued on to the Nez Perce village of Chief Kowesote for the winter. There Meek made a marriage alliance with Virginia, one of the chief's daughters. Her sisters were the wives of Newell and Wilkins. Meek's first wife had been killed in an Indian scrimmage and left him alone with their baby daughter, Helen Mar. Now he again had a complete family and would not risk taking them with him to the unsafe trapping area he planned to head for in March.

CHAPTER 12
1839

WASHINGTON, DC

President Van Buren's popularity had not increased. The country's depression continued. Many people turned to the government for help but were refused all public aid.

"The less government interferes, the better for general prosperity," was Van Buren's motto.

He was accused by antislavery leaders of driving the Seminole Indians out of Florida, which could cause a new slave state. He was attacked by pro-slavery leaders for not admitting the Republic of Texas as a new slave state.

The Texas vote to join the United States was opposed by northern states and by France and Great Britain, who feared it would aid the United States in gaining control of the southwest.

Boundary disputes with England continued in the Maine area, and the unsettled boundary question remained in the Oregon Country.

In spite of all the problems, Van Buren felt certain that he would be nominated for re-election by the Democratic Party.

GREEN RIVER

Pierre Chouteau had purchased the American Fur Company, and it was spring before he made his decision to send a supply train to Green River. It was a small caravan, headed by Moses Harris: four two-wheeled carts, each drawn by two mules, with about fifty mules and horses carrying the remainder of supplies. Twenty-seven people accompanied the train, including two missionary couples.

They began their journey on May 4 and rested one day at Fort Laramie (old Fort Williams) before continuing on in good weather toward Green River. Not knowing where on Green River the people would be gathered, Harris sent men ahead to locate the site. They returned with Andrew Drips and Joseph Walker, who guided them in, and they arrived at Horse Creek on July 5.

Indians and trappers had begun gathering near the mouth of Horse Creek in June, awaiting the supply train. Some of the trappers, including Kit Carson, had sold their furs elsewhere but had come to the meeting for the fun and fellowship. Fifteen Hudson Bay men from Fort Hall came. Joseph Meek came alone. He and a partner had trapped their way to the Tetons, where his partner was killed by the Blackfeet. Meek had escaped but lost his furs. Robert Newell was there and returned to Fort Hall with the Hudson Bay party and the missionaries on July 9.

The supply train left shortly after with Drips back in charge, leaving Moses Harris to spend the winter in the mountains. Before departing, an agreement was made to bring a supply train again the next year.

It was August before the last of the trappers left, including Kit Carson and Joe Meek. Meek was on his way to Salt River to continue trapping.

MISSOURI

Joel Walker, his wife, Mary, and his sister-in-law Martha Young were on their way home after spending the day shopping in Independence. As they rode along, Martha remarked how much the country had changed since they had first arrived in Missouri. As she remembered, there was nothing but wilderness then. Perhaps, she continued, it was time to load the wagons and move on. Mary and Joel agreed.

What began as simple conversation came up again and again in the days that followed. Other people in the neighborhood became interested, and when Joel heard that Andrew Drips was back and planning to take another caravan to Green River in the spring, he suggested they sell their farms and get ready to head west.

He told Martha and Mary that even if no one else decided to go, they could trail with Drips to Green River, where they would stand a good chance of encountering his brother Joe. They could go with Joe to California. If Joe wasn't at Green River, the group could surely find an Indian guide who would help them find their way.

The women agreed, and Joel began preparing for departure in the spring. He would sell their farm, and he and his wife, their four children, and his sister-in-law would head west.

FORT VANCOUVER

The fort burst into a festive celebration. The doctor had returned from his yearlong trip to Europe, and returning with him was his youngest son, David. After fifteen years, mother, father, and three of four siblings were reunited.

The family separation had begun when McLoughlin was assigned to the Columbia post. The two oldest children—John Jr., twelve, and Eliza, ten—were left in school in Montreal under the guardianship of the Frasers.

John Jr.'s school years were unhappy. In his late teens, he was sent to France and lived for a time with his uncle Dr. David McLoughlin. There he had enjoyed a fast life but did not do well in school. He returned to Canada and lived with various relatives, including his sister Eliza, who by then was married to William Randolph Eppes.

Two years ago, John Jr. had accepted an offer for employment from Governor Simpson and was sent to Vancouver, where he was reunited with his parents and his sister Eloisa. David was attending school in Europe at that time.

Shortly before McLoughlin had left on his trip, another festive celebration had occurred at the fort. His tall, blonde, fashionable daughter "Princess Eloisa" had married young, Scottish, handsome William Glen Rae, a new clerk at the post. Now Eloisa and William were the parents of a son, John.

A multitude of guests had gathered to greet the returning chief factor. While Eloisa and Margaret offered their guests English candies, cakes, and coffee, McLoughlin attempted to greet each person personally.

James Douglas had done an admirable job supervising the fort while he was away, and later, when they were in private surroundings, McLoughlin would relate to him and other staff members the successful negotiating that had been accomplished with the Hudson Bay House in London.

The plan they had developed for an agricultural company separate from the fur company had been approved. There would be two farm establishments. The Cowlitz Farm would be located near the Cowlitz River Landing. The Nisqually Farm, located near Fort Nisqually, would be headquarters for both establishments. The company would be known as the Puget Sound Agricultural Company and would be managed by Dr. William Tolmie.

The farms would be stocked with all farm implements and with livestock currently owned by the Hudson Bay Company: horses, cattle, sheep, swine, and goats.

Also approved was McLoughlin's plan to expand their salmon industry at Fort Langley and to continue developing the lumber trade in the Willamette Valley.

And receiving enthusiastic support was his proposal to establish a post in California at Yerba Buena on San Francisco Bay. Great Britain's claim to the Pacific Northwest had been strengthened to the north with the addition of Fort Stikine and Fort Taku. It was believed a post in California would strengthen their claim to the south. Governor Simpson was opposed to the California post but yielded to the authority of the company.

All of this could wait, however. Today the doctor would relish the warm and loving atmosphere of home and family and friends.

FORT HALL

Joe Meek's son, Courtney Walker Meek, was born at Fort Hall.
Meek missed the birth. After leaving Rendezvous in August, he had
found trapping at Salt River a poor hunt. When another trapper
came through and told him that Robert Newell; Newell's wife and
two children; Meek's wife, Virginia; and his daughter, Helen Mar,
were all at Fort Hall, he left to join them.

Arriving at the fort, he found they had all gone on to Fort
Crockett. He returned to Green River to spend the winter with
other trappers, not knowing that Newell was bringing the families
back to Fort Hall for the birth of Virginia's child.

WASHINGTON, DC

Lt. John C. Fremont was on his way to dinner at the home of
Senator Thomas Hart Benton of Missouri. The two had spent the
same evening at a hotel twenty-six years earlier, but of that evening
Fremont had no recollection, having been an eight-month-old baby
at the time.

It had happened in Nashville, Tennessee. Fremont's mother was
the daughter of a socially prominent Virginia family. She married
young and unhappily and in 1811 left her husband and ran off with
a handsome Frenchman, Charles Fremont. John Charles was born
in January, 1813, and in September the family was spending the
night at the City Hotel.

Andrew Jackson was also in Nashville that night, looking for
Thomas Hart Benton, then a young lawyer, whom Jackson claimed
had insulted his honor.

Jackson found Benton in the hotel corridor and began lashing
him with a horsewhip. Jesse Benton, Thomas's brother, came down
the corridor behind Jackson and shot him in his left shoulder. In
the melee that followed, a bullet went through a wall and narrowly
missed baby John. Jackson was rescued, and the Benton brothers
escaped unharmed.

When he was sixteen, Fremont entered Charleston College,
where he excelled and had an occasion to meet a South Carolina

politician, Joel Poinsett. Poinsett had served as the US ambassador to Mexico in the 1820s. In 1836 he became secretary of war and among other things organized the Army Corps of Topographical Engineers. Appointments to the Corps were highly sought at West Point; however, Poinsett had no problem obtaining an appointment for Fremont.

Fremont was assigned survey work in the upper Mississippi Valley under the supervision of Joseph Nicollet, considered the best topographer in the country. After the survey was completed, the men returned to Washington to the office of Nicollet to work up their report.

Senator Benton visited the office one day and met Fremont. The two men soon discovered they had a mutual passion for American expansion into the West: Down with the national bank! Down with slavery! On to the Pacific Ocean! Manifest destiny!

Tonight, dressed in his finest, handsome John Fremont was about to meet Benton's family, including his beautiful fifteen-year-old daughter, Jessie.

CHAPTER 13
1840

══

FORT VANCOUVER

After weighing the alternatives, McLoughlin made his decision. His son-in-law Rae had been promoted by the company to chief trader and assigned to take over the post at Fort Stikine. Fort Stikine, located on a strip of land leased from Russia, was an isolated, dangerous post.

Rae would take Eloisa and their son, John, with him. He would need a competent, loyal assistant. McLoughlin knew of no one who met those qualifications better than his son John Jr. John had done exceptional work since coming to Fort Vancouver. He and his brother David enjoyed being with each other, and they both adored their sister Eloisa.

It was hard for McLoughlin to break up the family again, but, feeling he was making the best decision, he assigned John Jr. to Fort Stikine as Rae's assistant.

Before they left with James Douglas, who was to escort them to the post, he warned the men, "Be master. Avoid offense. Deal honestly. Be kind. Be patient. But always expect an attack. Trust nothing to chance."

Willamette Valley

The last members of the Peoria Party arrived in the Willamette Valley in April. Jason Lee, on his way east in 1838, had met Thomas J. Farnham. Farnham became enchanted with Lee's stories of the Oregon Country and organized a party of eighteen men from his hometown of Peoria, Illinois, to go to Oregon for colonization.

They set out in May 1839 on their mounts with a few mules carrying their supplies. Unguided and with the Oregon Trail not clearly marked, the group soon ran into problems. At the Osage River, three men turned back, and three others joined a caravan heading to Mexico. A few stopped to winter with the trappers at Green River. Farnham and two of his men continued on, reached the Whitman Mission in September, and received guidance down the river to the Willamette Valley, where seven of the men who had wintered at Green River joined them in April.

The men who made up the Peoria Party were not trappers. Some were adventurers, and some were business-minded, like Robert Moore. Moore had been a major in the War of 1812 and after that a businessman in Peoria. He had left his wife temporarily in Illinois, hoping to get established immediately in Oregon so she could join him. One of the few immigrants who recognized that Indians had prior claim to Oregon property, Moore began looking around for a tribe to do business with.

Farnham, who had spent the prior rainy winter in the valley, was disenchanted with his trip, with Oregon, and with his plan for colonization. He made preparations to return east and write a book: *Don't Go West*.

Fort Vancouver

Dr. McLoughlin was surveying the Columbia River one afternoon when he saw a lone canoe approaching. As it drew closer, he recognized the single oarsman as Jason Lee. Jason Lee? Coming upriver in a canoe? How strange. He rushed to the dock, where Lee stepped from the canoe and explained that the ship *Lausanne* would soon arrive with his new wife and several newly recruited missionary couples. He had come on ahead to notify the doctor.

While in the east, Lee had been urged by his friends and associates to remarry and not return to his post alone. Anna Marie's parents were opposed to a new marriage. Mrs. Pittman pleaded, "Please do not take another wife until you have at least seen my daughter's grave."

Jason had answered that Anna Marie would have wanted him to remarry, and on July 26, 1839, he married Lucy Thompson, recently graduated from college and eager to do missionary work.

Among the new missionaries were Rev. and Mrs. Gustavus Hines, Rev. and Mrs. Alvin Waller, and George Abernethy, newly appointed financial manager for the mission.

The ship docked at six in the evening. McLoughlin, with Pastor Lee, greeted the arrivals and graciously invited them to the fort for meals and lodging until they could make their way up the valley to the mission.

Dr. Elijah White booked return passage on the *Lausanne*. White had been at the mission nearly three years. He was feeling restricted and confined, with unpleasant feelings toward Lee, so he took this opportunity to return to the east.

GREEN RIVER

Andrew Drips arrived at the last Rendezvous with thirty carts and forty men from the American Fur Company. Three hundred Shoshone warriors gave a parade to greet the train. Another group of Indians were there to meet Catholic Father Pierre Jean DeSmet, who had come to do missionary work among them.

Three Protestant missionaries and their wives had joined the train with two wagons of their own and would remain in camp pending guidance on to Fort Hall.

Joel Walker and his family, with their two wagons, had traveled with the caravan to the headwaters of Green River. There they received word that Joe was not at Rendezvous. They left the trappers and, with French-Canadian Jandreau as their guide, headed directly for Fort Hall. The Walker family had changed their plans since leaving Independence. Mary was pregnant. The trip to Oregon, from all accounts, was shorter and safer than the trail to California. Plus they were quite assured they would receive a warm family welcome from Mary and Martha's cousin, Ewing Young.

Father DeSmet stayed four days before he left with his group. After resting a few days, the other missionary families continued on in their wagons for Fort Hall, guided by Robert Newell and Joe Meek.

The camp showed some activity, but not like previous years. The fur business was dying, and Rendezvous was dying with it.

WILLAMETTE VALLEY

It was mid-September when the Joel Walker family arrived at the Ewing Young farm. Young was amazed at their story. They had stopped briefly at Fort Hall to rest and restock supplies and were advised by members at the fort not to take their wagons with them, because no one else had ever done it.

"Then we'll be the first," Joel said.

And they were. They were successful in bringing the wagons all the way to Fort Walla Walla, where they left them and arranged passage down the river by boat.

Ewing welcomed them into his home. "Can use some help," he told them. "Good you're here."

FORT HALL

Newell and Meek had safely escorted the missionary families to the fort in July. There the missionaries sold their wagons to the Hudson Bay Company in exchange for reliable mounts to finish their journey.

Meek spent a month at the fort with his family before reluctantly leaving to work the Snake River. In September he received a message from Newell asking him to come back to Fort Hall. Meek immediately packed his gear and left, arriving at the fort on the twenty-second.

"Come," Newell greeted him. "We are done with this life in the mountains."

A messenger had brought word of the Walker family taking their wagons all the way to Walla Walla. Newell had repurchased the missionary wagons and proposed they take the wagons and their families and do the same.

"What do you say, Meek? Shall we turn American settlers?"

Five days later, with their families and the wagons, they were on their way.

WILLAMETTE VALLEY

The Newell-Meek families arrived in the Willamette Valley on December 15. They had rested briefly at the Whitman Mission, where Dr. Whitman met them with joy and enthusiasm.

"You have proven wagons can be brought all the way. Now more people will come. Soon the area will be filled with Americans."

When Meek suggested he temporarily leave his daughter, Helen Mar, at the mission for schooling, Narcissa agreed. The Whitmans were still grieving the death of their own daughter and only child, two-year-old Alice Clarissa, who had wandered off and drowned in the river the previous year.

The party went on to Fort Walla Walla, where they left their wagons and continued on down the river in the rain to the valley.

CHAPTER 14
1841

WASHINGTON, DC

Thomas Hart Benton was angry. He hadn't been this enraged since the night he was horsewhipped by Andrew Jackson. "You married John Fremont?" he screamed.

Jessie had tried to prepare herself for his wrath. Now her long skirt hid her trembling knees. She raised her head higher to still her quivering chin.

Her mother intervened. "Thomas, it's done. There's nothing you can do about it now."

Yes, it was done. Jessie had fallen in love with John the first night he came to dinner. And he had admired her striking figure and her dark hair and eyes. *She's too young for me*, he thought. But as the year went on, he came to also admire her sensibility, her tenderness, and her keen mind. The romance grew, and a year after they met, they secretly slipped over to Senator John Crittenden's home one afternoon and were married. Jessie returned home, and more than a month had passed before she summoned the courage to tell her parents.

Benton was well aware of the special qualities his daughter possessed. He had been thinking she would be a good match for the president, fifty-seven-year-old widower Van Buren.

He continued to pour out his rage. Jessie stood her ground until, finally, Benton said he could accept the union if they agreed to make their home with him and the rest of the family.

WILLAMETTE VALLEY

Four months had passed since the Joel Walker family arrived in the valley. Joel had staked out a land claim and put up temporary housing for his family. He and his oldest son had been hired by Young to do farmwork, and Young had hired Martha to sew him some shirts and do his housework.

On January 14, Mary gave birth to a baby girl, Louisa. Mother and daughter were doing fine.

FRENCH PRAIRIE

A month earlier, the Joel Walker family had been celebrating the birth of Louisa. Today they were mourning at the funeral of their cousin Ewing Young.

They had made little contact with the other settlers in the valley until Ewing's sudden and unexpected death. His funeral had been arranged by Jason Lee, and all the settlers in the valley were in attendance.

After the funeral, Lee addressed the people, saying Ewing had no known heirs and he had left a sizable estate. Who was entitled to it? He went on to say that the need to legally dispose of an estate could arise again in the future, and he proposed that a committee be formed to better preserve the peace and good order of the settlements. He had prepared a proposed list of offices and a slate of candidates and, after some debate, it was agreed they would meet the next day at the Lee Mission House for further discussion.

WASHINGTON, DC

President Van Buren had been right. The Democrats did nominate him for re-election; however, his Senate-chosen vice president,

Richard M. Johnson, was so unpopular that Van Buren sought election without a running mate.

The Whig Party nominated William Henry Harrison for president and John Tyler as his running mate, both from Virginia. "Tippecanoe and Tyler too" was their campaign slogan. Harrison had received the nickname "Tippecanoe" after defeating the Shawnee Indians at the Battle of Tippecanoe in 1811. During the War of 1812, he was promoted to general. He resigned from the Army in 1814 and since had held various political jobs. Tyler, too, had held various political jobs, including governor of Virginia.

Harrison and Tyler won the electoral vote by a landslide. It was a cold, rainy day in Washington when Harrison gave his inaugural speech. He caught a cold, which developed into pneumonia, and he died on April 4, 1841.

John Tyler took over as president on April 6.

FORT VANCOUVER

Eloisa, her two-year-old son, John, and her new baby daughter, Margaret Glen, arrived safely by boat at the fort. Eloisa was delighted to be home again. The year she had spent confined at Fort Stikine, unable to leave it for safety reasons, had been dreadful—dark and drab.

When Eloisa and her husband received word he was being assigned to open a new post in California, they were delighted. He left immediately to set up the post. She waited for passage aboard the steamer *Beaver* and while sailing down the coast gave birth to Margaret Glen. When they reached Fort Nisqually, she was taken to the home of Mr. and Mrs. John Work, where she rested for three days before resuming her journey, riding a horse and carrying her new baby. At Cowlitz Landing, a boat was waiting to take them to the fort. She was now awaiting word from Rae as to when he would have quarters established so she could join him.

She wished her brother John could join them, but he had been placed in charge of Fort Stikine with a capable assistant.

SODA SPRINGS

Just beyond Soda Springs, the trail would divide, one branch leading north to Fort Hall and the other to California. There the Jesuits-Bidwell-Bartleson-Chiles wagon train would break up, some going to Fort Hall (and from there to the Snake Country or the Willamette Valley) and the rest going to California.

John Bidwell had come to Missouri in 1839 from the East Coast. He had claimed a piece of land and taken a teaching position, but when his land was taken away due to his having been under the age of twenty-one when he claimed it, he began reading and thinking about California.

He united with a few others who were also intrigued by California stories. They prepared and distributed literature under the name Western Emigration Society. Enquiries came in by the hundreds. People from various states agreed they would meet at Sapling Grove in May, properly outfitted and ready to go. Then Thomas Farnham, leader of the Peoria Party, published his book *Travels in the Great Western Prairies*, which presented an extremely bad review of life on the trail and advised would-be emigrants to stay home. Many took his advice. Bidwell arrived at Sapling Grove in May expecting to see five hundred wagons assembled for departure to California. There was one.

When the scheduled departure date came, forty-five more people had arrived. They came from different states, including Kentucky, Illinois, and Missouri. Some brought wagons. Some came penniless. There were young men seeking adventure, a few families, and a few businessmen. The largest family, the Kelseys, included five women and seven young children. John Bartleson, a fifty-four-year-old farmer from Missouri, brought eight men with him.

When Bidwell, now twenty-two, was asked if he knew the way to California, he replied, "Yes! We go west!" One of the group members had heard there was a party of Jesuits coming their way with Thomas Fitzpatrick as their guide; he suggested they wait and ride with them. Bidwell was reluctant to wait but was overridden by a company vote.

The Jesuits were headed by Father DeSmet, who was taking a second group to work with the Snake Indians. He had hired Fitzpatrick to guide them as far as Fort Hall and welcomed the Bidwell train to accompany them.

The combined group left on May 12, and a few days later, the Jesuits left them for a two-day detour to visit with a Kansa chief. The Bidwell party used the time to organize and elect officers according to the rules of the Western Emigration Society. Bidwell assumed he would be elected captain of the group, but Bartleson announced he felt he was the best man for the position—and stated that if he were not elected, he would take his eight men and leave. He was elected.

Five days later, they were back on the trail and overtaken by six men and one wagon. The leader of the men was Joseph Chiles, a neighbor of the Walkers in Missouri, who had been enticed to head for California after reading reports by ranch owner John Marsh.

Three days after that, Joseph Williams, a Methodist minister, rode into camp. He had traveled from Indiana to join the train, missed them at Sapling Grove, and ridden alone to overtake them.

As they approached Soda Springs, Fitzpatrick urged the Bidwell-Bartleson party not to go to California. The trail was unmarked, and dangers lurked along the way. Some of them agreed with him and said they would go on to Oregon. The majority elected to continue on to California. Fitzpatrick sent a messenger to Fort Hall to see if Joe Walker was there and would consent to guide them. Walker was not there, so the party voted to continue on their own.

CALIFORNIA

It was September when the Joel Walker family arrived by ship in San Francisco. They had stayed on in the Willamette Valley, continuing to work their land claim, after the death of Ewing Young. They had watched the disposal of Ewing's estate, some of it by auction, with Joe Meek acting as paid auctioneer. The organization meetings had continued under the leadership of Jason Lee, but no decisions had been made.

When Joel received word by messenger from August Johann Sutter asking him to become the manager of his farm in California, he accepted. The family was now preparing to continue up the Sacramento to Sutter's farm.

In November, the Bidwell-Bartleson party miraculously arrived at Marsh's Fort in the San Joaquin Valley. After parting from Fitzpatrick in August, they headed for Salt Lake, where they lost their way until friendly Indians came to their aid. One by one, they had abandoned their wagons, and when wildlife for food was nonexistent, they ate their oxen. At times they met Indians who fed them, and at other times they were followed by groups they feared were war parties.

When they reached the Humboldt area, the two leaders had a disagreement. Bartleson and a few of the men stormed on ahead. Some in the Bidwell party wanted to turn back to Fort Hall. A vote was taken, and by a narrow majority, they went on. Later the two parties were reunited and nearly starved going over the Sierra Range.

At the end of October, without knowing where they were, they reached the San Joaquin Valley, and a passing Indian told them Marsh's Fort was nearby.

John Marsh had arrived in Los Angeles in 1836, evading his arrest for running guns to the Sioux. He passed himself off as a doctor until he raised enough money to buy a large ranch in the San Joaquin Valley, where he accumulated herds of cattle and horses. Fearing the Mexican government would take his property away, he began to lobby for US annexation of California by sending letters to acquaintances and newspapers praising the wealth and beauty of California.

When the American party arrived at his fort, they were given food and supplies but also presented with a large bill. His settlement was not the beautiful place he had portrayed in his letters. The group dispersed quickly to find better locations.

Nancy Kelsey, the only woman who had elected to stay with the California group, made it safely with her year-old child. She was a strong woman and said, "I will not be separated from my husband."

About one hundred other Americans resided in California. Some were sailors who had deserted their ship, and the rest were ex-trappers.

August Sutter was now the most influential man in northern California. Following his plan, he had reached Fort Vancouver in 1838 and spent some time with James Douglas before going on to the Sandwich Islands. There he obtained an abundance of cargo, hired eight young men from the islands to go with him, and obtained passage on a boat sailing for California by way of Sitka, Alaska.

After obtaining a good return on his cargo, he contacted Governor Alvarado and requested a land grant, proposing to establish a settlement of Swiss families. Working with the governor, Sutter secured a large, choice area of land between the Sacramento and Feather Rivers, which dominated the inland waterways from San Francisco Bay. Besides the eight island men he had brought with him, he hired three white assistants and one Indian and began building an empire. His plan included a large adobe fort surrounded by a courtyard. There would be a village of shops, houses, mills, and warehouses where blacksmiths, flour millers, bakers, carpenters, gunsmiths, and blanket makers would carry out their trade. He would have no problem locating skilled workers, as numerous men in the country had lost their workplaces with the closing of the missions.

His kingdom in the wilderness would be as grand as Dr. McLoughlin's. Like the doctor, he would be a benefactor to all who came to him in need.

It was December when Eloisa arrived in Yerba Buena by ship along with her two children, her father, and Governor Simpson.

Shortly after Queen Victoria had knighted him at Buckingham Palace in January, Governor Simpson began a journey around the world, traveling by ship, horse, and canoe. When he reached Fort Vancouver in early spring, he arranged for James Douglas to accompany him, and they sailed for Fort Stikine.

As the influx of American settlers along the Columbia grew,

company officials became apprehensive that Fort Vancouver might be included in American territory when the pending boundary settlement was accomplished. Therefore, one of Simpson's assignments was to consider moving Fort Vancouver to a more British-controlled site. As their ship rounded the southern end of Vancouver Island, the two men agreed it looked like an advantageous site.

They went on to Fort Stikine and found everything operating smoothly under the direction of John Jr. Therefore, needing a man for Fort Simpson, Simpson took John's assistant, Finlayson, with him and replaced him with a man, McPherson, chosen from the group of French-Canadian and Hawaiian employees at the post.

It was late November when Simpson and Douglas arrived back at Fort Vancouver. Simpson briefed McLoughlin on the site they had selected for relocation and gave him orders to have a fort built on Vancouver Island and transfer all company property there as quickly as possible. First, however, they would accompany Eloisa and the children to Yerba Buena.

When they arrived, Dr. McLoughlin assisted the family in getting settled while Simpson inspected the post and the surrounding country. McLoughlin was pleased with the post. Simpson was not. He felt the location was poor. Rae was extravagant. Mexico exacted unfair customs duties.

The Raes, however, were delighted with their transfer. Yerba Buena was small: twelve houses, the company store, and a sawmill. The Spanish residents befriended them. They were invited to dinners and dances. It was a welcome change after their time at Stikine.

CHAPTER 15
1842

WASHINGTON, DC

There was a wedding at the White House. President Tyler's daughter Elizabeth was married, and Tyler's wife, Letitia, who suffered a paralytic stroke prior to their move into the White House, made her first public appearance.

The Tylers had now lived in the White House for ten months. They had not been enjoyable months. Back in 1827, when Tyler had been elected to the United States Senate, he had resigned and withdrawn from the Democratic Party rather than support the policies of President Andrew Jackson. He had accepted the nomination as vice-presidential running mate of Harrison with the Whigs Party, believing the Whigs had dropped their fight for a national bank and protective tariffs. Not so. When he became president after Harrison's death, Congress quickly passed bills calling for a new Bank of the United States and for higher tariffs. Tyler vetoed the bills. That night protesters surrounded the White House shouting insults and hurling rocks. When he vetoed a second bank bill, he was burned in effigy and received threatening death letters.

Tyler refused to give in to threats. He went calmly about his duties. He was a gentleman from Virginia with a strong mind of his own.

FORT VANCOUVER

Dr. McLoughlin and Governor Simpson spent two months in California before sailing to the Sandwich Islands. Their disagreements grew. McLoughlin boarded a ship for Oregon immediately upon arrival in Honolulu, leaving Simpson to inspect the company's installations there.

Upon McLoughlin's return to Fort Vancouver, he sent Douglas with a team of six men to Fort Nisqually with orders to board a company vessel and go to Vancouver Island to select a site for construction of the new fort.

ONTARIO, CANADA

Ranald MacDonald had a plan. Without telling anyone else what it was, he filled a small bag with clothes and a few books and walked away from Saint Thomas.

Ranald was the son of Scottish Archibald MacDonald of the Hudson Bay Company and Princess Sunday, the daughter of Chinook Chief Comcomly. Born at Fort George in 1824, he moved with his father to the new post at Vancouver the following year. His mother had died shortly after he was born, but he was soon to have a stepmother, Jane Klyne. He attended school at Fort Vancouver and at the age of eleven was sent to Canada to attend the newly opened Red River Academy. In 1839 he went on to Saint Thomas to live with the Edward Ermatinger family and serve as an apprentice at Edward's bank.

He enjoyed the social life in Saint Thomas, but his job as a bank clerk was boring. What he wanted to do was go to Japan. During his boyhood years, living at Fort Vancouver, three Japanese sailors had been shipwrecked off the Pacific coast, rescued and brought to the fort. The men had been aboard a ship sailing along the Japanese coast with a cargo of rice and porcelain dishes for delivery to the Shogun in Edo. A turbulent storm hit their ship, washing away its mast and rudder. The ship drifted for fourteen months. By the time it reached the Oregon shore, only the three young men, having survived on their cargo of rice, were still alive.

Remembering the features of the three men, Ranald often wondered if perhaps his mother's ancestors had also come from Japan. If so, the sailors were his kin. He wanted to visit their country, to know more about their people. It was an impossible dream. For more than two hundred years, Japan had cut itself off from the rest of the world. One Dutch ship was allowed to come to Nagasaki once a year, but no one was allowed to leave the ship. Japanese people were not allowed to leave their country, and no foreigner was allowed to enter their country.

But today eighteen-year-old Ranald had a plan. He, like the three Japanese sailors, would become shipwrecked off the coast of Japan, be rescued by the Japanese, and brought safely into their country.

FORT STIKINE

John McLoughlin Jr. penned a letter to his father. It contained an ominous note. He explained that McPherson, his new assistant, had proven to be inexperienced and ineffective. A large amount of liquor had been brought into the fort a few days earlier. His attempts, with no assistance, to control his employees had failed. They were angry.

He finished his letter, "I know the men will kill me tonight. I will die bravely. Like a man."

Five days later, Simpson and his entourage arrived from Honolulu. They found the flag flying at half-mast, the fort in chaos, and young John McLoughlin dead.

Simpson interviewed four men. One man confessed he had fired the shot that killed McLoughlin. Weighing the testimony he received, knowing there was no criminal jurisdiction in this strip of leased Russian land, and anxious to be on his way, Simpson made his decision quickly.

He said it appeared from the testimony that both the murdered man and the murderer were drunk. Any court trying the case would find a verdict of "justifiable homicide." Therefore, he would have the man who made the confession accompany them to Sitka, where he would be released with no charges.

MISSOURI

At Elm Grove, twenty-five miles southwest of Independence, an emigration train was preparing to leave for Oregon. There were sixteen wagons and one hundred and five people, of which fifty-one were males over eighteen. The train had been organized by Dr. Elijah White. His neighbor in New York, Medorem Crawford, was in the group, along with Lansford Hastings, Amos Lovejoy, Sidney Moss, Osbourne Russell, and Stephen Meek (older brother of Joe Meek).

Since his return to the East, White had made contact with Senator Lewis Linn from Missouri, who was pushing for United States sovereignty over the Oregon territory, even if it meant going to war with Great Britain. White, with his inside knowledge of the country, was offered the position of subagent for the Oregon Indians, a position which included Secret Service financing for Western movement of emigrants. That is, funding would be provided for newspaper advertisements featuring the glories of the West, along with salaries for caravan guides if a caravan were organized.

White accepted the position and was successful in attracting people as he made his way from the East Coast to Independence, promoting Oregon as he traveled.

To run an orderly caravan, he decided there should be an election of officers. He proposed a captain, a guard, secretary, blacksmith, and wagon maker, along with a "White's Code of Caravan Laws"—which included, among other things, no obscene conversation or profane swearing.

He assumed he would be unopposed for captain, but Lansford Hastings, a young man from Ohio, ran against him. White won by a very narrow margin, which caused the voters to insist on a fresh election each month.

The train left Elm Grove early on the morning of May 15 in

good weather. The wagons, with their snow-white coverings, were followed by a long train of horses, mules, and cattle with whistling drivers walking beside and behind them.

The people were happy and filled with anticipation. They were on their way to Oregon!

FORT VANCOUVER

It was June before Governor Simpson's letter telling of John's death reached Fort Vancouver. As the doctor read the letter, his emotions turned from disbelief to grief to anger. The governor, he felt, had made a decision that not only pardoned a guilty man, but charged his son with poor character and misappropriate behavior.

Simpson had concluded his letter by telling McLoughlin to say nothing of the matter to anyone else. The company did not want unfavorable publicity.

McLoughlin's anger increased as he reread the letter. He vowed to ignore Simpson's request for silence and do everything in his power to bring the murderers to justice and set the record straight.

WILLAMETTE VALLEY

Jason Lee wrote a letter to Mr. and Mrs. Pittman explaining he had prepared a box of Anna Maria's personal items to ship them some time ago. He had tried three times to ship it, but it had not been accepted for lack of space. It was now at Fort George and would be sent soon.

He said he had been extremely busy and now had no one to share his sorrows. His wife, Lucy, had died.

"On February 26 our daughter was born and three weeks later her mother died. The Rev. and Mrs. Gustavus Hines are caring for baby Lucyanna.

"I am disappointed that I have never heard from you. Let me know if you ever need any help from me."

WHITMAN MISSION

Elijah White's caravan was straggling in. Problems had plagued them all along the way. Three days after leaving Elm Grove, White had become annoyed with the barking of the dogs and decreed that all dogs in camp be shot. This had made him very unpopular with all dog owners, and when the first month was up, Hastings won the election for captain. Amos Lovejoy was elected his deputy. The election caused a split in the party. White rushed ahead with his loyal group, and Hastings, left with the cattle group, was unable to keep up.

There were deaths along the way and some minor Indian problems. At Fort Laramie, the two groups reunited, and White, using his Secret Service funds, hired Thomas Fitzpatrick to guide them to Fort Hall.

A new Hudson Bay man, Richard Grant, was in charge at Fort Hall. Grant, like other company employees, was under orders not to encourage American settlers. However, he welcomed them, let them purchase supplies, and tried to discourage them from taking their wagons any farther.

The caravan spent eight days resting at the fort. Grant drew detailed maps and supplied local guides to get them to Fort Walla Walla.

White's party arrived at the Whitman Mission two days ahead of Hastings's party. White delivered a letter to Dr. Whitman from the Missionary Board. The train went on to Fort Walla Walla and from there would make the perilous river journey to Fort Vancouver, where, on up the Willamette Valley, Dr. McLoughlin had surveyed and founded a new settlement at the Falls called Oregon City.

Marcus Whitman was shocked by the letter White brought him from the Missionary Board. It contained orders for him to close the missions in the West. His first thought was to start back east immediately and attempt to get the orders rescinded. Then he thought about Narcissa. Winter was coming on. He couldn't leave her alone at the mission through the winter. However, when he discussed the matter with her, she agreed it was a matter that could not be left unattended until spring. She had good help and assistance at the mission, she said, and he should leave for the East as soon as possible. Amos Lovejoy, who had remained at the mission, offered to return with him. The two left on October 3.

MISSOURI

Joseph Chiles was back in Missouri and had opened a new business as an emigration agent and guide to California.

In April he and a dozen men had met at Sutter's Fort and planned their return trip from California to Missouri. They went first to Los Angeles, and then back to northern California, on to Fort Hall and Green River, and then southeast to the Santa Fe Trail and followed it back to Missouri, mapping as they went. They reached Missouri in September, and Chiles immediately made arrangements to open his business, hoping to have a train ready to leave in the spring.

CHAPTER 16
1843

WASHINGTON, DC

President Tyler was grateful to his daughter-in-law Priscilla Cooper Tyler for serving as White House hostess. His wife, Letitia, had passed away the previous September.

His personal sorrow had deepened, and his popularity in political circles had not increased. He had vetoed more bills passed by Congress. Henry Clay, Whig leader in Congress, had finally given up and resigned. The Whigs had attempted, but failed, to have him impeached.

He favored annexation of Texas as a slave state but was opposed by northern congressmen, including John Quincy Adams, who was serving his twelfth year in Congress.

CALIFORNIA

Joel Walker and his family made a decision to return to Oregon. They had spent a year and a half in California. The children needed schooling and were encountering a language problem. While serving as manager of Sutter's farm, Joel had acquired a sizable herd of cattle and horses. Arrangements were made for the women and children to return by ship, and a crew of drovers was hired to assist Joel and his son in taking the animals overland.

In Yerba Buena, Eloisa Rae had given birth to a daughter, Maria Louisa. It was not going well for her husband. The market for hides and furs was diminishing. A severe drought had resulted in crop failures, and he was not able to ship contracted wheat to consumers. Further, he did not fully understand the intentions of the company regarding their policy in California. He wrote Governor Simpson for instructions. In return, Simpson contacted McLoughlin and ordered him to close the post. McLoughlin, still bitterly opposing Simpson over his account of John Jr.'s death, ignored the order.

WILLAMETTE VALLEY

Philip Foster; his wife and four children; Mrs. Foster's brother Frances W. Pettygrove; Pettygrove's wife and child; and four other people from the East arrived in Oregon early in the spring. Pettygrove and Foster were businessmen in Maine who had made contact with Jason Lee when he was on his recent trip to the East Coast. After listening to Lee talk about Oregon, they saw a great opportunity. They sold their businesses and booked passage aboard a ship in New York. They sailed around the Horn and wintered in the Sandwich Islands, where they stocked up on supplies for the store they planned to open. From the islands, they came up the Columbia River as far as the ship could take them and then finished their trip up the Willamette River in canoes. They found property along the river, and the men immediately began construction of a three-story building. As soon as the ground floor was completed, they opened for business.

On July 4, they gathered with other people from the valley at Champoeg. Settlers came in farm carts, missionaries came on horseback, and gentlemen and their ladies from Fort Vancouver came in canoes. Men, women, and families came. They pitched their tents and partook of shared food and festivities in celebration.

The following day, they all solemnly gathered to adopt laws to govern themselves, prefaced with "We, the people of Oregon Territory, for the purpose of mutual protection, and to secure peace and prosperity among ourselves, agree to adopt the following laws and regulations until such time as the United States of America extends their jurisdiction over us."

More than two years had passed since the funeral of Ewing Young. The committee appointed at that time had made slow progress. Some members had resigned, with new ones appointed to replace them. Opinions differed.

Dr. McLoughlin had operated the area under the laws of the British-Canadian government. The Hudson Bay trappers who had settled in the upper Willamette Valley favored continuing this type of government.

The Methodists, being the majority of Americans, felt they should be in control of establishing a government.

Another element was added when the Catholic missionaries arrived.

When Dr. Elijah White arrived in the valley, he announced that since he had been appointed subagent of Indian Affairs, his office should be considered equivalent to that of governor of a colony.

All this was cause for chaos and confusion when the group met at Champoeg on May 2. After a vote was taken, there was a fifty-fifty tie between Americans and Canadians, with two men undecided, until Joe Meek stepped forward with a stick in his hand, drew a line in the sand, and shouted, "Who's for a divide?"

Whether it was his commanding appearance, his authoritative voice, or the size of the stick, the two undecided members joined the Americans. A probate judge, A. E. Wilson, was then elected. Wilson in turn appointed a committee composed of both Americans and Canadians to draft a provisional code of laws for the territory, such laws to be presented for consideration on July 5.

OREGON AND CALIFORNIA

The trails to Oregon and California had bustled all summer. John Fremont, on his second surveying assignment, had left Jessie with her family and started out from Missouri in May with thirty-nine men and Kit Carson as guide. Fremont's written assignment was to extend his prior survey to the Pacific Ocean.

Joseph Chiles had successfully recruited a group for California. He began the trip with Fremont but soon became dissatisfied, and he and his group pushed on alone.

The largest group was made up of more than a thousand people who arrived in Independence in the early spring. Some came with wagons loaded with provisions. Others brought with them herds of oxen and cattle. There were businesspeople like Peter Burnett, who had convinced his creditors that he could successfully fulfill his financial obligations if they would wait until he got to Oregon. The Applegate family had both education and wealth. William Overton from Tennessee was in the group. Some freeloaders tagged along. Some farmers, used to solitude, were stressed by the noise and crowds. There were men quick to draw their guns. There were women and children. All were attracted to the West by what they had read and heard, but the majority of them came because word was out that a bill had been introduced in Congress allowing 640 acres of free land in Oregon, even though it was still a territory under the joint occupation of two nations.

The group organized themselves as the Oregon Emigrating Company and elected John Gantt, who had never been west, as their guide. They left on May 22, traveling in separate trains. The cattle train, with nearly two thousand head of cattle led by Jesse Applegate, were the last, as they moved the slowest.

It was early July when the first group reached the South Platte River and Dr. Marcus Whitman caught up with them. He had arrived late and missed the train in Missouri, but had overtaken them by traveling fast on horseback. He was not welcomed by leader Gantt but very welcomed by the majority of the train. Not only did he know the way, but now they had a doctor available who also possessed a soothing manner.

As Fremont's party neared Fort Hall, Kit Carson went on ahead and purchased supplies. Fremont then turned and headed for the Salt Lake area.

Chiles was nearing Fort Hall when he met Joseph Walker and engaged him to guide his group on to California from the fort.

As the parties converged on the fort, trouble ensued. Richard Grant, still in charge of the post, had sold most of his supplies to

Fremont's party and to the first arrivals of the Oregon Company. When the last trains arrived, including the Chiles party, he had only enough food left to get his own employees through the winter. He refused to sell any more but changed his mind when some of Chiles's men threatened him.

The Oregon Company dismissed John Gantt at the fort and replaced him with Dr. Whitman. Gantt, angry, left the group and joined up with Chiles.

Grant, as he had done previously, discouraged the company from taking their wagons any farther. Whitman, knowing that Meek and Newell had been successful, overruled Grant, and most of the train continued on with their wagons, heading for the Columbia River.

Whitman was anxious to get to The Dalles, where Narcissa was to meet him. So, once over the mountains, he left the train in the hands of a competent guide and rode on ahead. The Dalles was located below the mission, at the confluence of the Deschutes and Columbia Rivers.

In June, Narcissa had felt she was near the breaking point and, taking Helen Mar with her, had gone to Fort Vancouver to see Dr. Barclay. The doctor prescribed iodine for her and at least a month's rest at the fort. She reluctantly agreed, knowing she was missing important developments in Champoeg. After her month of rest, she and Helen Mar went on to the mission for a visit with Joe Meek. In October, Jason Lee escorted them back to The Dalles, as he was eager to see Whitman and hear the news from the East.

Whitman was shocked when he was reunited with Narcissa and realized the seriousness of her condition. He also was weary and limping from his 6,000-mile trip. His good news was he had been successful in convincing the board to keep the mission open. His bad news was he had heard the Methodist Board planned to recall Jason.

They went on together to the mission, and Whitman was shocked again when he found the vanguard of the train had arrived and broken into their house; the mission had become a chaotic inn; and the emigrants were clamoring for supplies.

Whitman provided what he could and sent the train on to Fort

Walla Walla. McLoughlin, hearing of their urgent need for supplies, sent two boatloads of free provisions up the river. Wagons were disassembled and rafted down the river. People were loaded into boats. There were mishaps, and some lives were lost. The cattle were driven overland through the mountains. Late in October, families began reaching the valley. Others didn't arrive until November.

The new arrivals soon bought out Foster and Pettygrove's supplies. They sent off an order to E. and H. Grimes in Honolulu asking that every item on their previous list be doubled.

Robert Moore had been successful in his negotiations for a tract of land from the Indians. It was across the river from McLoughlin's claim. He had built a cabin on the hillside and called his domain Robin's Nest. He envisioned that someday, it would have a mill, stores, and homes on lots he would sell. However, when he saw the number of new settlers arriving, he sent an order off to the Sandwich Islands for tents.

Meanwhile, the Chiles party had reached the Humboldt Sink, where twenty-five people, including women and children, had been left with their wagons under the guidance of Walker while Chiles and thirteen of his men, with an Indian guide, took horses and left for Sutter's Fort to get supplies. They arrived at the fort in the middle of November, but, believing the return route would be impassable by then, did not attempt to go back. Walker, however, was able, after abandoning the wagons, to find a route. He got the rest of the party safely to Sutter's by the end of December.

The construction of Sutter's Fort was complete. The massive adobe fort had walls eighteen feet high and two feet thick. The courtyard was large enough to muster an army of a thousand men. The village contained shops, houses, mills, and warehouses. It was a haven for arriving Americans.

Fremont spent several days measuring and surveying the Great Salt Lake and vicinity. He considered this one of the great points of the exploration, but his men grumbled over having to eat seagulls, roots, and grasses to keep up their strength. When they returned to Fort Hall and discovered the other travelers had cleaned out the fort's supplies, their grumbling grew louder until Fremont gallantly offered to pay off those who did not want to continue. Eleven men accepted the payoff and headed east. The rest continued on toward Fort Vancouver. When they reached the Whitman Mission, they were able to purchase some potatoes, and at Fort Vancouver, McLoughlin sold them flour, peas, and other supplies they needed.

Fort Vancouver was as far as Fremont had been assigned to explore, but after collecting topography information and mapping and determining the heights of mountains in the area, he gave the order to continue south, toward California.

FORT VANCOUVER

James Douglas returned to the fort in December. He and his men had spent most of the year on Vancouver Island. The building of Fort Victoria, the name chosen for the new site in honor of the queen, was now complete. He was prepared to work closely with McLoughlin during the upcoming transitional period of moving the company from Fort Vancouver to Fort Victoria.

Chapter 17
1844

"What hath God wrought?" The first public telegraph message was tapped out by fifty-three-year-old Samuel Morse and sent from the Capitol of the United States to Baltimore, Maryland. Spectators looked on. It was a momentous day.

Morse was born in Charleston, Massachusetts, into a devoutly Calvinist family; his father was a minister. He attended Yale, where he studied chemistry. He found lectures and experiments on the science of electricity amusing and instructive, but his passion was art. He was nineteen when he graduated and convinced his reluctant parents to send him to England to continue his studies at the Royal Academy of Art. He had some success there; his clay model of Hercules won him a gold medal. In 1815 he ran out of money and returned home.

To support himself, he began painting portraits. Again, he had some success. He did many portraits, one being of Marquis de Lafayette, and in 1822 he did a painting depicting the House of Representatives. When he heard that four huge paintings were to be included in the rotunda of the Capitol in Washington, he returned to Europe to prepare himself to apply for the work. He stayed in Europe for three years.

Returning home aboard the ship *Sully*, Morse was at dinner one evening when he heard men discussing the possibility of transmitting intelligence by wires using electricity. An idea came to him. The rest of the trip he spent making notes and drawing pictures of his telegraph plan, reasoning that if he obtained the rotunda paintings position, he would make enough money to support himself and still have time to continue perfecting the telegraph.

John Quincy Adams was a member of the committee selecting artists. He believed American artists were not good enough for the job. Morse was denied the position and relegated to living in a room on the top floor of his brother's newspaper building with a job at the City of New York University as teacher of painting and sculpturing. Still, he did not give up on his project. He bought wires in pieces, soldered them together, wrapped the wire with cotton thread, and built his instruments from old clockworks and art equipment.

Leonard Gale, chemistry instructor at the school, became interested in Morse's project. Together they studied the work of Joseph Henry, a physicist at Princeton University, and based on his work built an electromagnetic telegraph.

Alfred Vail, a student at the university, also became interested in their work. Vail's father owned an iron and brass works in New Jersey. Vail offered to build a sturdier model. Morse accepted the offer and gave Vail a one-fourth partnership. They experimented by stringing ten miles of wire around Morse's workroom and sending coded messages using dots and dashes.

Morse took the new model to Washington and requested a grant from Congress to test the telegraph. Congress refused. He took it to Europe and France and found no support. He came back to America and, still unable to find financial backing, was about to give up when, on the last night of the 1843 session, Congress passed a bill appropriating $30,000 to test the telegraph.

On May 24, 1844, the successful test was made. Morse once again looked forward to wealth and fame.

NEW YORK CITY

President John Tyler and Julia Gardiner were married in a June wedding in New York. A few weeks earlier, Tyler had been cruising on the USS *Princeton* to observe the firing of a new naval gun. The gun exploded, killing David Gardiner and five other people. In the aftermath of the tragedy, Tyler met Gardiner's daughter Julia. They were attracted to each other and soon decided to be married.

MISSOURI

First Lieutenant John Fremont and his party returned to Saint Louis in July after a grueling fourteen-month journey. After leaving Fort Vancouver, they traveled south to Klamath Lake. Weather was bad. They were stalked by Natives who did not openly attack them but at times stole horses. Other tribes were friendly. In January, a tribe gave them food, and one of their young men agreed to guide them across the mountains. The snow was heavy and slippery; at times the men crawled on their hands and knees to make a path for the animals. Some of the men were deranged from the hardships by the time they reached Sutter's Fort in March. Sutter outfitted them with new animals, and they set out again. Six weeks later, after crossing the Mojave Desert, Joseph Walker overtook them. Fremont hired him as guide.

Fremont mapped as they went on to Bent's Fort and at last back to St Louis. Jesse was awaiting him, and they immediately went to work on a 600-page report that included guidebook information on traveling west. More than 10,000 copies were published. Fremont received a promotion to captain.

OREGON AND CALIFORNIA

Six parties had assembled in Missouri in the spring. Starting at four different points, they all planned to reach Fort Hall and then branch off for Oregon or California. Over 1,500 people left in May with wagons, provisions, and livestock.

Rains were unusually heavy during May and into June. Rivers

flooded and covered the prairie with water. Fights broke out over food and disagreements with the leaders. There were constant signs that Native war parties were assembling. There were illnesses and deaths.

At Fort Hall, the California parties continued on to their southern destination. It was December before they reached Sutter's Fort.

The Oregon parties pushed on for the Willamette Valley. Both parents of the seven Sager children died, and when the wagons reached the Whitman Mission, the children were left with Marcus and Narcissa. By the end of the year, the population in the Willamette Valley had increased by 1,400.

Robert Moore's Robin's Nest was now a village of tents and had been renamed Linn City in honor of Senator Linn, who had introduced the land bill into Congress.

Philip Foster and Francis Pettygrove were doing a good business in their store in Oregon City. One day an Indian visited the store and told Foster about a farm for sale fourteen miles east on Eagle Creek. Foster checked it out. The man who had claimed squatter's rights to the land wanted to sell. Foster bought the land, built a cabin on it, and moved his family to Eagle Creek.

Dr. McLoughlin continued to assist with services and supplies, even though complaints against him were rising. He had been successful in keeping Americans out of the area north of the Columbia River, but now the press of circumstances was such that he could hold them back no longer. A group of seven men, five of whom had families, hovered close to Fort Vancouver for a time and then moved on up to Puget Sound. He had refused settlers' requests to buy cattle. The company, developing their farm, needed every available animal to increase their herds. This caused more complaints. Threats were made to set fire to Fort Vancouver. McLoughlin sent word to London asking for protection. The reply he received was to protect the company's interests as best he could.

In addition to his work at the fort, he had been developing the land at the Falls by having a gristmill, a sawmill, and three houses built. He had the land he called Oregon City resurveyed by Sidney

Moss and again by Jesse Applegate. Part of the land was plotted into blocks and lots. Some lots he sold; he made gifts of other lots for church buildings and a school. However, a complaint arose that the company held a monopoly on the Willamette Valley, and claim jumpers and members of the Methodist mission began occupying land that he claimed.

CHAPTER 18
1845

YERBA BUENA

A woman from the Mission Dolores was at the home of Eloisa Rae, attempting to comfort her. Eloisa stared out the window, feeling no emotion. She had no emotion left. A week ago, she had been in bed, resting after the birth of her second son four days earlier.

Her husband was with her. His extremely agitated manner caused her to ask him if he had problems.

He replied that he had so many, he was going to kill himself.

She pleaded with him until he put a pistol to his head and walked into the next room. She heard a gunshot.

Today, a week later, her baby son had died. She continued to stare out the window.

WASHINGTON, DC

Once again a cold, steady rain soaked the unpaved streets of Washington as the city prepared for another presidential inauguration. James Knox Polk was about to take the oath.

Polk, whose mother was the great grandniece of Scottish

Protestant Reformation leader John Knox, was the oldest of ten children.

When he was eleven, his family moved from North Carolina to Tennessee. After graduating at the top of his class from the University of North Carolina, he entered the law office of Felix Grundy, who introduced him to Andrew Jackson. He and Jackson, both Presbyterians, became close friends, which earned him the nickname "Young Hickory." He was elected to the Tennessee House of Representatives, where he supported Andrew Jackson's presidential ambitions. In 1825 he was elected to the US House of Representatives, where he opposed all policies of President John Quincy Adams. When Jackson was elected president, Polk became Speaker of the House. In 1839, with Jackson's backing, he became governor of Tennessee.

Polk had not planned to run for president. In 1844 he was merely a delegate at the Democratic Presidential Convention. Former President Van Buren was the leading candidate. Van Buren's chief rival was Lewis Cass from Michigan, former US minister to France.

When agreement had still not been reached on the eighth ballot, George Bancroft, delegate from Massachusetts, proposed Polk as a compromise candidate. Polk received unanimous approval and accepted the nomination, declaring that if he were elected president, he would discharge the duties of the office for one term but would not be a candidate for re-election.

His opponent was Whig candidate Senator Henry Clay. Polk was referred to as a "dark horse," or little-known candidate, and the Whig campaign slogan became "Who is James K. Polk?"

The big political issue was the annexation of Texas. Clay did his best to avoid the issue, while Polk stated openly that both Texas and Oregon had always belonged to the United States by right and called for the immediate reannexation of Texas and for the reoccupation of the Oregon Territory.

Polk won the election.

CANADA

Jason Lee passed away at Stanstead, Canada, the home of his youth, not knowing the Oregon mission he created had been repudiated and destroyed.

Upon receiving the word from Marcus Whitman that the board was sending George Gray by ship to investigate charges raised against him of critical performance and careless bookkeeping—and, if necessary, to replace him, Lee had resigned his position.

He left his daughter with the Hines' and immediately sailed east to answer the charges in person. Hearings held during the summer of 1844 exonerated him, but he was too weak and worn by then to return to Oregon. Instead, he headed back home to Stanstead.

Gray, upon arrival in Oregon, soon determined the organization was no longer fulfilling its purpose and sold everything at bargain prices to former mission members.

FORT VANCOUVER

Eloisa Rae, her son, John, and her two daughters, Margaret and Louisa, arrived safely by boat at the fort in April.

Immediately upon receiving the news of Rae's death, Eloisa's brother David had booked passage to California to escort her and the children home.

When Eloisa saw her parents faithfully awaiting the boat's docking, she vowed she would never leave them again.

WASHINGTON, DC

President Polk settled into the White House. His wife of twenty-one years, Sarah Childress, took over the position of secretary to him. He appointed his staff. Among them was George Bancroft, whom he made Secretary of the Navy. He confided to Bancroft the four goals he had for his term in office: reduce the tariff; re-establish an independent treasury; settle the Oregon boundary dispute with Great Britain; acquire California.

The annexation of Texas was already under way. Three days

before Tyler left office, he had signed the House and Senate joint resolution admitting Texas as a state.

Today, however, was a sad day. Polk had received word that his friend and colleague Andrew Jackson had fallen unconscious at his home in Nashville. When he regained consciousness, his slaves were crowded around him, weeping. He told them not to cry—that they would all meet in heaven. That evening, he died.

WILLAMETTE VALLEY

The new colonists had succeeded in making changes in the organic laws, and on August 15, John McLoughlin and James Douglas agreed to support the amended laws. They took an oath to uphold the laws of the provisional government of Oregon as far as the said organic laws were consistent with their duties as a citizen of the United States or a subject of Great Britain.

McLoughlin wrote the company, explaining why they had done this. "We have yielded to the wishes of a respectable part of the people in the country, of British and American origin, by uniting with them in the formation of a temporary and provisional government designed to prevent disorder and maintain peace until the settlement of the boundary question. We decided on joining the association both for the security of the Company's property and the protection of its right."

Dr. McLoughlin received a stern reply from Governor Simpson ordering him to complete the company transfer from Vancouver to Victoria at once.

WASHINGTON, DC

President Polk, working with his wife, attempted to sort out messages regarding the new state of Texas, the potential state of California, and the country of Oregon.

A messenger had arrived with word of a dispute over the boundary between Texas and Mexico. Even though the United States had annexed Texas, Mexico refused to give up its claim or agree to a boundary for the new state. Texas claimed the boundary line was the Rio Grande River; Mexico claimed it was the Nueces River.

He also had word that both American and Mexican residents in California were unhappy with being governed by Mexico City and were about to declare their independence. He had conferred with John Fremont before Fremont left on his third surveying expedition with Joseph Walker as guide. Polk reasoned they would now be somewhere in the Great Salt Lake area, heading for California, where Fremont would view the situation and forward information. Another rumor was that England was about to buy California from Mexico.

Diplomatic relations with Mexico had been completely severed when Mexico recalled its minister from Washington following the annexation of Texas. At that time, Polk had dispatched John Slidell as envoy to Mexico with instructions to make a cash offer of $25 million if they would accept the Rio Grande as boundary for Texas and sell New Mexico and California. He was waiting for word back from Slidell.

Regarding the Oregon country, Polk's campaign slogan had been "54–40 or fight." In his inaugural address, he stated the United States had clear and unquestionable title to Oregon. Now talk of war with England was sweeping the country. He knew the influx of Americans into Oregon was increasing, and that General Stephen Kearny and his troops stationed at Fort Leavenworth were patrolling the wagon trails to ward off Indian attacks. If England declared war, Kearny would have to be notified immediately. He needed fast, reliable communication.

Would that Morse's telegraph lines were stretched across the country!

OREGON CITY

Sam Barlow and his wife reached Oregon City on Christmas Eve. They were among the three thousand people who left Missouri in the spring heading for California and Oregon. Sam Barlow came from Kentucky. His wife, Susannah Lee, was kin to "Light-Horse Harry" Lee and Robert E. Lee, both military men. Sam and

Susannah had grown children who accompanied them. Barlow headed up a train in association with a train headed by Joel Palmer, a young man from Indiana.

When Barlow's train reached The Dalles, it was late in September. No boats were available to take them down the river. Rather than wait, he proposed to blaze a wagon trail over the mountains. He was told it was impossible, but he set out with seven wagons.

A few more days passed before Palmer and his train arrived at The Dalles. Along the way, Palmer had visited with General Kearny; had stopped at Fort Boise, where he met Elijah White, who was going east to collect his salary as Indian subagent and lobby for an appointment as governor of Oregon; and stopped at the Whitman Mission to visit with the Whitmans. When he arrived at The Dalles and heard Barlow had left overland with his wagons, he and his train immediately set out following their trail and caught up with them where they had made camp.

The people from the two trains made plans. They built a cabin, called Fort Deposit, where they planned to store their goods and wagons and go on to Oregon City by horse. Barlow and a man from his train then started overland to blaze a trail. Several days later, they staggered down a slope into a flat near Eagle Creek, where two of Philip Foster's young boys were herding cows. The boys were terrified when they saw two men in rags with long, straggly beards calling to them. They rushed home to tell their father. Foster took the men to his house and gave them food and aid.

Some of the people at Fort Deposit followed the blazed trail and made it to Oregon City by the end of October. Others returned to The Dalles and found passage down the river. Barlow returned to Fort Deposit and made arrangements for one of his men to remain and guard the property. He and his wife went back to Foster's farm, where they rested for some time before proceeding on to Oregon City.

CHAPTER 19
1846

OREGON CITY

D r. and Mrs. McLoughlin moved into their new home in Oregon City with their son David, their daughter Eloisa, and her three children. McLoughlin had resigned from the Hudson Bay Company at the end of the previous year, leaving it in the hands of James Douglas.

He had pursued his private investigation into the death of John Jr. until John was vindicated by the London officials, but no reprimand was given to Simpson. He and Simpson disagreed also on the land acquired and developed at Willamette Falls. McLoughlin claimed it was acquired as the result of a mandate issued by the London Committee. Simpson declared McLoughlin acquired the property for himself, not for the company, and McLoughlin was forced to repay the company for all expenses connected with the development. Disagreements abounded over other matters until the London Committee informed McLoughlin he would have to get along with the governor or leave the company.

McLoughlin faced his problems with determination and energy. He resigned but stayed on at the fort until his large, pretentious home in Oregon City had been completed.

WASHINGTON, DC

President Polk found his problems increasing. He received word that Mexican officials had refused to allow John Slidell to present his cash settlement proposal. Thus, on January 13, he dispatched an order to General Taylor to advance with his three thousand men from the Nueces River to the Rio Grande.

Word received from the Oregon Country indicated tension continued to mount over the settlement of the boundary line. British warships were reported seen in Puget Sound and on the Columbia River.

Another concern regarded the Mormon congregation. Joseph Smith, who founded the church in New York in 1830, had been killed in 1844 following their move to Illinois. Now his successor, Brigham Young, a carpenter from Vermont, had organized a wagon caravan and left Illinois planning to form a new settlement in the Great Basin area of the far West. If the situation with Mexico continued to intensify, Polk knew General Kearny's assistance would be required by General Taylor. Pulling Kearny from his current duty of patrolling the Western wagon trails would leave no law enforcement in the area. This could open the possibility of further hostile action toward the Mormons.

OREGON COUNTRY

John Fremont was biding time at Klamath Lake. He had reached California in February and immediately contacted the Mexican authorities. He told them he was on a surveying assignment in the interest of science and trade. Initially he was granted permission to stay in the country, but his welcome did not last long. The first week in March, he was ordered by General Castro to leave.

Fremont, insulted, marched his men to Hawk's Peak in the Gavilan Mountains and raised the American flag. Three days later, he reconsidered his action and retreated back to the Sacramento Valley. Joseph Walker looked at it as an act of cowardice, left his employ, and headed out for Southern California.

Fremont stayed in the valley for a time, awaiting orders or other news from Washington. When none came, he retreated back to Oregon Country.

WASHINGTON, DC

It was May when President Polk received word that on April 25 a Mexican force had crossed the Rio Grande River and defeated a small body of American cavalry. Immediately upon receiving the news, Polk asked Congress to declare war, stating Mexico "invaded our territory and shed American blood on American soil."

Congress declared war on May 13 as volunteers cried, "Ho for the Halls of the Montezumas!"

CALIFORNIA

Fremont waited at Klamath Lake until May, when he was met by Lt. A. H. Gillespie, who gave him a verbal message from Secretary of State Buchanan directing him to return to California to "watch and counteract any foreign scheme and conciliate the good will of the inhabitants toward the United States."

Lt. Gillespie did not have current news from Washington, so Fremont returned to California not knowing that war had been declared. He found General Castro had ordered all non-Mexicans out of California, which had caused American settlers to organize and take control of the village of Sonoma. They called themselves *osos* (bears) and referred to their action as the Bear Flag Revolt.

Fremont, his services having been diverted from the field of exploration to international issues, declared himself an officer in the Army and took over as their leader. He led a battalion of volunteers to Monterey, where he united with Commodore Robert F. Stockton, who was in command of the US Naval Forces at the port. Commodore Stockton promoted Fremont to the rank of major and sent him south to Los Angeles.

OREGON COUNTRY

After Samuel Barlow arrived in Oregon City, he made arrangements to appear before the Provisional Legislature to ask for funds to build a road on the trail he had blazed. Barlow had picked up his road-building skills from his father, who had helped Daniel Boone build a road through Cumberland Gap into Kentucky. With Philip Foster as his partner, Barlow was successful in obtaining a license and an advance. They hired forty men and began clearing and enlarging the trail. They soon realized the $4,000 advance was not enough to complete the job but continued on, buying supplies on credit that they planned to repay by charging a toll for passage over the road.

Reuben Gant brought the first wagon over the eighty-mile Barlow Road late in the summer, and J. W. Ladd, the first emigrant to drive his own wagon over the road, reached Oregon City on September 13.

In Oregon City, Dr. McLoughlin had found both friends and rivals. George Abernethy engaged in a conspiracy to force him to give up his land. Jesse Applegate and Peter Burnett continued to support him. Other people who still spoke highly of him were Fremont, Wyeth, Barlow, and Father Blanchet.

Early in November, a messenger from James Douglas arrived at McLoughlin's home and delivered good news. A peaceful agreement had been reached between the United States and Britain to set the forty-ninth parallel as the dividing line between the two countries, with the exception of Vancouver Island. The entire island remained British. The Hudson Bay Company was officially moving its headquarters from Fort Vancouver to Fort Victoria, and the United States was paying the company for their Puget Sound agriculture holdings. The agreement gave the Hudson Bay Company free navigation of the Columbia River and possessory rights within the portion of the land ceded to the United States.

WASHINGTON, DC

President Polk reviewed his year. He was pleased that the acquisition of Oregon had been acquired without bloodshed. The acquisition of California and Texas was still pending. Mexico, under the leadership of President Santa Anna, refused to negotiate. General

Taylor had succeeded in crossing the Rio Grande and now occupied the main towns in northeastern Mexico. General Kearny had been ordered to dispatch half of his men to the Rio Grande and proceed to California with the other half.

CHAPTER 20
1847

WASHINGTON, DC

The war with Mexico continued. Polk and his Democratic Party advisers decided the best maneuver was to attack Mexico City from the east. General Taylor's record of victories seemed to make him the best choice to lead the invading army; however, a presidential election was coming up, and the Whig Party was already talking of running Taylor as their candidate. Fearing the further growth of a popular Whig leader, they chose General Winfield Scott, veteran of the War of 1812, to lead the campaign.

Robert E. Lee was transferred to Scott's command because of his engineering skills. Lee, son of the leading family in Virginia and married to the great granddaughter of Martha Washington (Mary Ann Randolph Curtis), was a graduate of West Point and commissioned as a second lieutenant in the Corps of Engineers. At the start of the war in 1846, he was sent to Texas as assistant engineer under General John Wool, where he supervised the construction of bridges. His engineering skills would be used to advantage while crossing the difficult mountain passes to Mexico City.

Others assigned to General Scott's command were Benjamin

Bonneville, Ulysses Grant, William Sherman, George McClellan, George Meade, Stonewall Jackson, and Jefferson Davis.

Hoping for a speedy end to the war, Polk briefed Nicholas Trist from the State Department on acceptable provisions of an armistice and sent him to accompany Scott.

CALIFORNIA

Major John Fremont had been successful in capturing Los Angeles without a battle. One of his men dated a letter February 6, 1847, in Yerba Buena: "Nearly the whole of the immigration have been off with Fremont who has command of all the land forces."

Commodore Stockton promoted Fremont to lieutenant colonel.

MEXICO

General Scott landed his troops and began his advance toward the capital on March 9. Meanwhile, Santa Anna had learned of their plans and attacked General Taylor. Although the Mexican forces outnumbered them, the Americans were successful in winning the battle. When the news reached the States, Taylor was proclaimed an American hero, and talk grew of his being the next president.

CALIFORNIA

General Kearny left California with Lieutenant Colonel John Fremont as his prisoner. Shortly after Kearny had arrived in California, a feud had erupted over who was in command. Kearny had written orders to proceed to California; Fremont's orders were oral. When Fremont declared he was under the command of Commodore Stockton, Kearny arrested him on charges of disobeying orders, mutiny, and conduct to the prejudice of good order and military discipline. Kearny was taking him back to the States to have him court-martialed.

SALT LAKE VALLEY

Brigham Young had changed his plans for the destination of his followers. While traveling they had met Father DeSmet, who told them about the great Salt Lake Valley.

Following the maps of John Fremont, they traveled along the Platte River to Fort Laramie. The main group camped at Green River while a small number went on to Fort Bridger and then to the Salt Lake Valley, where they began irrigating the land in preparation for sowing of crops.

WASHINGTON, DC

President Polk received word that General Scott had landed his troops and begun his advance toward the Mexican capital on March 9. After fighting battles along the way, Scott entered Mexico City on September 14.

When the word was out that the old Aztec Indian "Halls of Montezuma" had been captured, American masses clamored for annexation of the whole of Mexico.

OREGON COUNTRY

Members of the Cayuse tribe gathered for a meeting. They had watched as wagon after wagon of migrating whites crossed their land, bringing death with them.

"Our people die from the white man's disease. We have gone to Whitman for medicine. It does not help. They still die."

"The white men do not die. They go on in their wagons. Does Whitman give them better medicine?"

"Whitman should be killed, as our medicine man would be if he made our people die."

"No, we cannot kill Whitman. He came to help us."

The meeting continued into the night. The young men grew angrier until the older men could no longer reason with them.

It was nearly midnight when Dr. Whitman arrived home. He had gone during the day to answer a call for help from a lodge up the river. After treating the sick Indians, he hurried back. The last of the wagon trains had left a few days ago. Some of the people had been too ill or tired to go on and would stay at the mission for now.

He had been looking forward to a night of rest, but he found Narcissa still up, watching over Helen Mar and Louise Sager, who were very ill. She was exhausted, and he sent her to bed while he took up the watch. When morning came, she arose and made him some breakfast, after which he went outside to arrange for the butchering of a cow.

Once the job was under way, he came back into the kitchen, sat down in a chair, and fell asleep until a knock came on the door.

Two young Indians were there, asking for medicine. When he turned to comply, one struck him with a tomahawk. The other one shot John Sager, who was in the room, and when Narcissa came to see what the trouble was, she was also shot.

A group of Indians then surrounded the people who were camping at the mission. Twelve of the men were killed, six escaped, and the remainder—consisting of thirty-four children, eight women, and five men—were taken hostage. Helen Mar and Louise Sager were left unattended.

It was the sixth of December before news of the massacre reached the Willamette Valley. Peter Ogden was at Fort Vancouver and, with sixteen men accompanying him, immediately left for Fort Walla Walla. Once there, he summoned the Cayuse chiefs to a meeting.

He advised them that an army of men was being assembled in the Valley, and the only way to avoid attack was to release the hostages. As encouragement, he offered to pay them $500 in merchandise.

The Cayuse, urged by the Nez Perce, accepted the offer and released the hostages to Ogden.

The Provisional Government attempted to raise an army of 500 men, but they had little authority or money. They realized their few volunteers would be vastly outnumbered by the Indian population. The colonel of the group was thus ordered to declare to the Indians that this was not war but an expedition to capture the murderers of those slain at the mission.

CHAPTER 21
1848

═══════════════════════════

CALIFORNIA

It was a mild January in California, and James Marshall had been sent by his employer, John Sutter, to the south fork of the American River to begin construction of a sawmill.

Marshall had lived in his home state of New Jersey until he decided to go west to Oregon. He had ended up in California at Sutter's Fort, where his carpentry skills landed him a job.

It was the twenty-fourth day of January when he discovered gold nuggets in the river. He rushed back to the fort and gave Sutter the news. In spite of their excitement, they agreed to keep the discovery a secret.

MEXICO

Santa Anna resigned after the fall of Mexico City. The new government was receptive to ending the war and met with Nicholas Trist in Guadalupe Hidalgo, near Mexico City, where a settlement was negotiated. The treaty required Mexico to give up the territory Polk had originally asked for: the Rio Grande region, New Mexico, and California. The United States paid Mexico $15 million for the territory.

Washington, DC

John Quincy Adams was at his House desk on the twenty-first of February when he suffered a paralytic stroke. He was too ill to be moved from the building and was carried to the Speaker's Room. He had served in the House of Representatives for seventeen years. His last words before he died two days later were, "This is the last of earth. I am content."

Oregon Territory

On the last day of February, the volunteer men organized by the Provisional Government reached the burned ruins of the Whitman Mission. The group included Joe Meek. They found the mission deserted. Wolves had dug bodies from shallow graves. They reburied the bones and returned home with their report.

The ruling government agreed they had to send someone back to Washington to present their appeal for military protection. Who better than Joe Meek? Besides his negotiating ability, he was a cousin of President Polk's wife.

Meek agreed to their request and was ready to leave by early March. A hundred volunteer soldiers escorted him and nine companions as far as the Blue Mountains. They were then beyond Cayuse territory. Their plan was to travel to the Bear River and along the Platte until they reached Missouri.

Japan

Six years had passed since Ranald MacDonald left Saint Thomas. He had gone on foot from Saint Thomas to the Mississippi River, where he found employment as a deckhand on a steamboat going to New Orleans. He sent his family a letter from New Orleans before he went on to New York and signed onto a ship bound for London. He had to serve for two more years as an ordinary seaman before he made it to Hawaii and found employment with Capt. Lawrence Edwards on the whaling boat *Plymouth*. Capt. Edwards was sailing for Japanese waters and agreed he would supply Ranald with a small sailboat and a few provisions and allow him to leave the ship off the coast of Japan in exchange for Ranald's share of the whaling venture.

In March they moved into Japanese waters, and by June the ship was ready to return to the States. They lowered Ranald's boat and left him alone at sea. He delayed making an appearance on land for three days, until the *Plymouth* was well out of sight.

It was early morning as he approached Rishiri Island and saw men coming his way in a skiff. He removed the drain plug on his boat until it was half filled with water. As the skiff approached, he frantically waved his arms and, using sign language, indicated his boat was sinking, and he needed to be rescued. His plan worked. He was greeted with friendliness, taken ashore to the headman's house, and made welcome.

WASHINGTON, DC

When Joe Meek arrived in Washington, worn and tired, President Polk and his wife received him immediately. Polk was sympathetic to his request. Meek was allowed to speak before Congress, which was debating the Donation Land Bill. Congressmen did not agree on the amount of acreage on which a person could file. Southerners suggested a thousand acres. Meek explained it was unrealistic to expect one man to develop a tract of land that size by himself. To slave owners, it would be a reasonable plantation, but in Oregon, 640 acres was more reasonable.

It was not until the last action before adjournment that Congress voted to make Oregon a territory. President Polk signed the bill on August 14. He appointed Joseph Lane of Indiana as governor. Lane had been born in North Carolina. He moved with his family to Kentucky when he was a young boy and later to Indiana, where he held political state offices until serving as an officer in the Mexican War.

Polk appointed Meek as United States marshal for the territory, then hurried the two men off with a detachment of soldiers, so they could return to Oregon and put the government into operation before Polk went out of office on March 4, 1849.

Since it was late in the season, a more southern route was chosen. They planned to follow the Santa Fe Trail and then go west to the Colorado River, into Los Angeles, and up to San Francisco, where they would catch sea passage to Oregon.

MISSOURI

In October, John Fremont and thirty-five men left Saint Louis to explore the terrain of the Missouri, Kansas, and Arkansas rivers. After President Polk had commuted his sentence of dishonorable discharge, Fremont had resigned his commission and, with the aid of Senator Benton, obtained financing for his expedition. Benton was seeking support from the Senate for a railroad connecting Saint Louis to San Francisco.

CALIFORNIA

The secret James Marshall and John Sutter had agreed to keep was out. News of the discovery of gold in California had reached Oregon. Joel Walker and his family were back in California. Peter Burnett organized a wagon company made up of 150 energetic men with fifty ox-drawn wagons loaded with mining equipment and provisions and left in September. They followed the route to Klamath Lake and from there searched for a route that would be passable for wagons.

They encountered serious difficulties when they reached the Sierra Nevada but were overtaken by a second party that had left from Puget Sound. They combined their efforts to make a trail to the Sacramento Valley before the snows of winter came.

SALT LAKE VALLEY

More than five thousand settlers had safely arrived at Great Salt Lake where Brigham Young had viewed the scenic land and said, "This is the place."

They laid out the streets of a city with streets running directly north and south or east and west. The dry desert land responded to their irrigation methods, and crops flourished. When hordes of crickets appeared and threatened to destroy the crops, flocks of seagulls came and ate the crickets. The grateful pioneers erected a monument to honor the gulls.

CHAPTER 22
1849

CALIFORNIA

The steamer *California* sailed through the Golden Gate into San Francisco Bay. Gold! Gold! Gold! The secret Sutter and Marshall had agreed to keep was spreading.

WILLAMETTE VALLEY

People began arriving at the Rose Farm, near the south edge of Oregon City, early on March 3. William and Louisa Holmes had settled on this land when they came west by wagon in 1843. A log cabin sheltered them until their home was completed. It was the finest home in Oregon City, and their 640-acre land claim was called the Rose Farm because of the many roses Louisa planted in her garden.

The residents of the area had been alerted that Joe Meek and Joseph Lane were in Oregon, and today Lane would declare Oregon to be a territory of the United States.

The people, dressed in their best, socialized in the front yard until the two gentlemen arrived. Lane wore his general's uniform, and Meek was equally impressive dressed in the suit his cousin Sara Polk had encouraged him to acquire when he was in Washington.

Governor Lane spoke to the people below from the balcony off the second story of the Holmes residence. After reading the proclamation, which began, "In pursuance of an Act of Congress, approved the fourteenth day of August in the year of our Lord one thousand eight hundred forty-eight, establishing a Territorial Government in the Territory of Oregon ..." he finished with his inaugural address, and Oregon was officially declared to be a territory of the United States.

The day ended with a barbecue meal followed by a formal ball, which lasted until dawn. Various issues were discussed as Lane mingled with the people. The one issue that received unanimous agreement was the need for roads.

WASHINGTON, DC

Sixty-five-year-old Zachary Taylor was inaugurated as president on March 5. The United States had been one day without a president, as Polk's term had expired on the third and Taylor had refused to be inaugurated on the fourth, a Sunday.

Taylor had not been interested in entering politics, and his wife was very opposed to it, but the Whig Party had nominated him, along with Millard Fillmore for vice president. They ran against Democratic Senator Lewis Case of Michigan and General William Butler of Kentucky. Former president Van Buren ran as a candidate for the Free Soil Party. Taylor and Fillmore won the election.

Taylor was the son of a Revolutionary War veteran who lived in Kentucky, where he had received a war bonus of six thousand acres of land. Zachary Taylor had fought in the War of 1812 and various Indian wars. In 1837 he received the rank of brigadier general and in 1846 was sent to the Rio Grande, where, during the ensuing conflict, he became a war hero.

JAPAN

The American ship *Preble* was anchored in the Japanese port of

Nagasaki in April. With the aid of Dutch negotiators, the *Preble* had been allowed to enter Japanese waters to retrieve thirteen seamen who had survived the shipwreck of an American vessel and were being held in Japan as prisoners. Due to the restrictions on foreign people in their country, the Japanese officials, to whom Ranald MacDonald had been entrusted, believed it safest for him to join the seamen and leave the country.

Ranald was in no hurry to leave. Shortly after his arrival on Rishiri Island, he was escorted to Nagasaki and confined. During his seven months of confinement, he was well treated and became a teacher. Fifteen men were sent to him to learn English. In turn, he learned the Japanese language. The men were able to engage in discussions about the outside world. He told them about Great Britain and America and Canada and explained the principles of constitutional government. As he communicated with his students, he had the feeling he had been made a teacher of English because the country desired changes. He believed the enlightenment provided through his conversations would reach the heads of government.

As he left his confinement to be escorted to the *Preble*, he thought, *So it happened, and all for the best! There* is *a Providence that shapes our ends.*

He whispered, "Sayonara."

CALIFORNIA

Gold-seeking hordes continued to pour into California. They came by ships from all parts of the world. Covered wagon caravans came. John Sutter's land was overrun with claim jumpers. He deeded part of it to his son, John Jr., who founded the town of Sacramento, which soon became a mining center.

Law-abiding citizens of California, including those with political experience who had arrived from the Oregon Territory, realized a state government must be erected. Working together, they drafted a constitution and applied to Washington for admission to the Union.

TENNESSEE

James Polk returned to his home in Nashville in March. As Polk predicted, President Taylor was not comfortable with the appointment of Joseph Lane as governor of the new Territory of Oregon. Taylor immediately began looking for a replacement. He first offered the position to a young Whig member of Congress from Illinois, Abraham Lincoln. Lincoln's wife had no desire to go west, and Lincoln declined the offer. An offer was then made and accepted by John P. Gaines, who had served under General Scott in the Mexican War.

Polk was pleased to be away from Washington but worn out by his four years of devoted duty. Within three months of his homecoming, he became ill with cholera and died on June 15.

WASHINGTON, DC

President Taylor, stressed with the duties of the presidency, listened as Senator Henry Clay urged him to work out a compromise over the slavery issue.

Since Taylor had taken office, what to do about slavery had been a main concern. With new states and territories being added to the Union, the question of whether slavery should be extended was hotly debated. He knew the Whig Party had assumed he favored slavery when they drafted him to run as their candidate for the presidency. However, he had never committed himself on the issue.

Now a petition from California had been received requesting admission as a free state. Southerners threatened secession if the petition was granted, while Northerners pushed for slave-free admission and promised war to preserve the Union.

Although Senator Clay recommended compromise, Taylor's mind was set. There would be no compromise. California would be admitted to the Union as a free state.

CALIFORNIA

While Californians awaited word from Washington on their statehood, the Mexican village of Yerba Buena was increasing in population. It was resurveyed and renamed, and the plat drawn up was labeled the official map of San Francisco. On November 9, the document was delivered to Capt. William Irving to be taken by vessel to Oregon City, the only incorporated town west of the Rocky Mountains, where the plat could be filed.

OREGON TERRITORY

Colonel William Loring and his regiment reached The Dalles in November after a long, hard trip. Congress had granted Oregon's request for military protection, and the first US Mounted Rifles had been ordered to proceed to Oregon City. They left in the spring with the understanding that Governor Lane would send a supply train to meet them at Fort Hall. That plan was foiled when the supply train met a band of Snake Indians near the Blue Mountains and was forced to turn back. By the time the regiment reached The Dalles, their supplies were limited, and both men and animals exhausted.

Loring and his officers agreed the safest plan was to send most of the men on to Vancouver by boat and leave a small command to take the wagons and animals overland by the Barlow Road. Due to cold weather and heavy snow in the pass, most of the animals were lost, and the command was forced to leave the wagons at a site they named Government Camp.

When the regiment that left the east with more than six hundred men reassembled in Vancouver, talk of the gold discovery in California was rampant. A third of the men deserted and headed south. The remainder of the regiment was established in temporary shelters on land behind Hudson Bay Company's Fort Vancouver.

Chapter 23
1850

Oregon Territory

As soon as Governor Lane had the government in operation, in his dual role as commissioner of Indian Affairs, he accompanied Colonel Loring and his detachment to the Cayuse tribe and demanded the surrender of the Indians guilty of the Whitman Massacre.

Five Cayuse men volunteered to return to Oregon City with them. The five men were accused of murder, and a trial began. The accused maintained they were innocent and that the ten men who had committed the Whitman crime had all been killed.

On the third day of the trial, the verdict "Guilty as Charged" was given, and the defendants were sentenced to "hang by the neck until dead."

On June 3, the hanging was carried out on the bluff above the Falls in Oregon City by Joe Meek in his capacity as US marshal.

Colonel Persifer F. Smith arrived with orders to construct permanent military quarters at Fort Vancouver. A military reservation was established in the area behind the British trading post, which was still operating with a skeleton crew, and construction of Columbia Barracks began under the supervision of Capt. Rufus Ingalls.

On June 18, knowing he was to be replaced, Lane wrote out his resignation as governor, accompanied an escort south to settle a dispute with the Rogue Indians, and then went on to California to prospect for gold.

Washington, DC

Vice President Millard Fillmore was sworn in as president of the United States on July 10. President Taylor had died the previous day.

Fillmore was from New York, born in a log cabin in Locke. His schooling was very limited, but when he was nineteen, he decided to become a lawyer. He received his training from a local judge and after practicing law for a few years was elected to the US House of Representatives, where he served until the Whigs nominated him as running mate for Taylor.

During his sixteen months as vice president, he had presided impartially over the Senate debate on the issue of slavery. When he became president, he came forth strongly in favor of compromise and promptly signed a series of laws passed by Congress called the Compromise of 1850. The compromise abolished the slave trade in the District of Columbia, admitted California as a free state with Peter Burnett as govenor, and organized the territories of Utah and New Mexico with no reference to slavery.

He also signed the Oregon Donation Land Claim. The act provided for establishment of legal title to the land in the Oregon Territory.

Prior to passage of the act, who the land actually belonged to had been in question.

The truth was spoken by an ex-trapper who had turned farmer: "As there are no laws in this country, we do the best we can."

People staked claims, farmed the land, laid out town sites, subdivided and sold lots, even resold their claims.

The Organic Articles and Laws drawn up for the Provisional Government were modeled upon the Northwest Ordinance of 1787 and the Statutes of Iowa Territory. Land claims were also based on the Linn Law, but the act passed on September 27, 1850, was unique to the Oregon Country.

It granted to every male over eighteen who was a citizen of the United States, having made declaration on or before the first day of December 1850, and who resided and cultivated the land for four consecutive years, the quantity of 320 acres of land, if he were a single man. If he were a married man, and his wife resided with him, she was granted 320 acres for a total of 640 acres. Those men settling in the Oregon Country between December 1, 1850, and December 1, 1853, who were over twenty-one and a citizen of the United States, would be allowed 160 acres if single. If these men were married and their wives resided with them, each wife would be allowed 160 acres for a total of 320 acres per couple.

CHAPTER 24
1851

OREGON TERRITORY

John B. Preston, his wife, and their daughter, Clara, arrived in Astoria along with five young women who had been sent by the Congregational Church Society to serve as teachers.

As soon as the Donation Land Claim had been passed, Oregon legislators rushed an appeal to Washington for an official survey to be made, so pioneers could establish definite boundary lines and obtain clear title to their land.

President Fillmore appointed Preston as surveyor general to do the job. When the ship docked in Astoria, Preston made immediate arrangements to get his group to Oregon City, where, after he had delivered the women to their destination, he planned to get his family settled, establish an office, and go to work.

By early May, he had his plan in place and had organized a survey crew. After visiting various locations, he had determined the point of intersection of the base and meridian lines. On June 4, he and his crew traveled up the steep grade of Tuality Trail and drove a cedar stake into the ground at that point.

Preston's duties as surveyor general included adjudicating claim disputes, establishing title to land claims, and verifying citizenship of claimants.

One of his cases involved Robert Moore of Linn City, who had purchased his thousand-acre tract from Chief Wanaxha. Under the Oregon Donation Land Claim Act, Moore had to file for lawful claim to his land. Since his wife had not joined him, he had to relinquish all but 320 acres.

NORTH OREGON TERRITORY

On August 29, settlers in the North Oregon Territory gathered in Cowlitz and prepared a memorial requesting that the US government divide the Oregon Territory. The reasons given for such a separation stressed the geographic isolation and inconvenience in travel that restricted participation in government affairs. To illustrate, it explained that it cost more and took longer for a North Territory citizen to travel to a clerk's office or district judge than it did for a man to travel from Saint Louis to Boston and back.

McLoughlin was successful in keeping American settlers from the area north of the Columbia River until 1844, when Michael Simmons led a small group, traveling by canoe up the Cowlitz River and then overland, to Puget Sound. With help from the Hudson Bay Company situated at Fort Nisqually, they built a sawmill and gristmill.

The following year, two men from New England, Levi Lathrop Smith and Edmund Sylvester, arrived and filed claims. Smith was elected to the Oregon Territorial Legislation but died in a drowning accident before he could attend his first session. Sylvester inherited the entire claim and in 1850 hosted a dedication ceremony for his land site.

One of his guests penned a poem that ended with the words

Olympia's gods might view with grace
Nor scorn so fair a dwelling place.

Sylvester chose the name Olympia for his site. He and his investors soon purchased the brig *Orbitt* and ran pilings sawed by Simmons's mill to San Francisco and returned with goods. As their business grew, the US government opened a customs house there.

On the Fourth of July, the settlers had gathered in Olympia to celebrate. The celebration climaxed with a speech by John Chapman extolling the benefits of establishing a separate government. His speech was well received, and the August 29 meeting was scheduled.

OREGON CITY

In September, John McLoughlin, after more than two years of waiting, became a full citizen of the United States. By then the land he had claimed in Oregon City had been taken from him. He was allowed to continue living in his home and was serving as mayor of Oregon City after winning forty-four of the sixty-six votes cast by adult male property owners.

Between 1846 and 1850, he had built houses, sawmills, and gristmills, providing employment for needy immigrants. He had given away three hundred lots for private and public use. His greatest honor came in 1847, when Pope Gregory XVI bestowed upon him the knighthood of Saint Gregory for his "upright life, correct morals and zeal for religion." The document and medal were delivered to him by Father Blanchet when Blanchet returned from a visit to Rome.

CHAPTER 25
1852

═══════════════════════════════════

OREGON TERRITORY

I t was early morning on a lovely spring day. Benjamin Louis
Eulalie de Bonneville viewed the landscape from his quarters
at Columbia Barracks. He had arrived three days ago and was
not adjusted completely to the realization that the facility he had
been denied access to seventeen years ago was now under his
command.

In the years following his western expedition, he had been
assigned to various military bases before serving in the Mexican
War. After the war, he was stationed at Fort Kearny until reassigned
to Vancouver.

Unrest stirred among the Indians in the area, but nothing that
demanded his immediate attention. Today he would arrange to
take a boat trip up the Willamette River. He had heard the new
town of Portland already had a population estimated at 700 and
boasted of more than fifty businesses and six industrial plants. He
wanted to see it for himself.

When he arrived at Columbia Barracks, he found his
quartermaster was Ulysses Grant, a young military man he met
when they were both engaged in the Mexican War. He decided to

invite Grant to accompany him on the boat trip as a good way to reconnect.

Portland, originally a pleasant wooded area on the Willamette River called the Clearing, was used as a stopping place for boats traveling between Oregon City and Vancouver. When William Overton arrived in 1843, he staked a claim, set up a tent, and was residing there when Asa Lovejoy returned to Oregon after escorting Marcus Whitman back east.

Lovejoy was on a canoe trip to Fort Vancouver when he stopped at the Clearing and met Overton. The Clearing was the point at which, in 1841, Capt. John H. Couch, skipper of the brig *Maryland*, made the observation that any ship that could get into the mouth of the Columbia River could proceed up the Willamette River to that point, but not as far as Oregon City.

Lovejoy accepted Overton's offer to sell him a half interest in his claim and envisioned a town on the site; Overton thought a small farm. Before a decision was made, Overton decided to move south and sold the remainder of his claim to Francis Pettygrove.

Lovejoy and Pettygrove worked together in clearing the land, plotted sixteen blocks, and built a log house and a store. They were in disagreement, however, over what to call their town. Lovejoy, from Massachusetts, wanted to name it Boston. Pettygrove, from Maine, wanted to call it Portland. At a dinner party one evening, they flipped a coin. Pettygrove won. Portland was the agreed-upon name.

In 1848, Pettygrove sold his share to Daniel Lownsdale and left for California. Lovejoy sold his holdings to Benjamin Stark. In 1851 Portland became an incorporated town. By the beginning of 1852, it was the principal port in Oregon.

WASHINGTON, DC

President Fillmore signed the Oregon Location Bill on May 4. This ended the disagreement over where the territorial capital should be located. The first sessions of the territorial legislature had been held in Oregon City. In February 1851, the legislature met there again. Before adjournment, they passed a bill declaring Salem the seat of government. Salem, located a few miles south of their original station, was plotted as a town by Jason Lee and the Methodist missionaries.

The bill passed by a narrow margin. When the session met again in December, Governor Gaines and three of the twenty-two members of the House refused to go to Salem and met in Oregon City.

The Oregon Location Bill established Salem as the official seat of government. The bill also transferred additional territorial functions to other towns, including Portland.

Oregon City lost much business because of the Location Act, and many of its citizens moved—principally to Portland, where ocean vessels now stopped and seldom continued upriver as they had in the past.

CHAPTER 26
1853

WASHINGTON, DC

Franklin Pierce had taken Fillmore's place in the White House. He had won the Democratic nomination for president in 1852 after a stalemate occurred among the four strongest candidates: Stephen Douglas, James Buchanan, William Marcy, and Lewis Cass. His Whig opponent was General Winfield Scott.

Pierce had served under General Scott in the Mexican War. Prior to the war, he served in both the US House of Representatives and the US Senate. After his nomination for president, he gained public support and won the election because he strongly favored the Compromise of 1850.

The campaign for the division of the Oregon Territory that began at Cowlitz in 1851 had continued, and shortly before President Fillmore's term expired, he signed the bill creating Washington Territory. It was now up to President Pierce to appoint the first officers.

When Pierce ran for president, Isaac Stevens campaigned for him and was rewarded with an offer for a political appointment. He chose and was granted the position of governor to Washington Territory.

Stevens, descendant of Puritan immigrants, had been born in

Massachusetts in 1818. After his graduation from West Point, he served in the Mexican War with Robert E. Lee.

Pierce appointed Jefferson Davis as secretary of war. Davis, also a Mexican War veteran, was very interested in having a railroad built that would run from the Mississippi River to the Pacific coast. Before this could be accomplished, organized engineer companies would need to explore and find the best location for a route. Davis requested that Pierce assign Capt. George McClellan to accompany Stevens to Washington Territory and survey the Cascade Range for road building. His request was granted.

Pierce, at forty-eight, was the youngest president to be elected. He and his wife suffered a great sorrow two months before his inauguration when their eleven-year-old son died in a railroad accident. His wife, unrecovered from grief, was not able to attend any social events and was still secluded in an upstairs bedroom while her aunt served as White House hostess.

Fort Vancouver

Quartermaster Ulysses Grant waited impatiently for his friends to join him. He had good news. He had received permission from Commander Bonneville to use land at the fort for their potato project. He had also purchased at a very affordable price a pair of old horses from a recently arrived immigrant. With the team, he could break up the ground, and they could begin planting. As they had discussed, inflated prices in the area assured them of a good profit, and they all agreed they could use more money than what the Army was paying. Grant planned to use his to bring his wife, Julia, and his two young sons out.

Grant, a northerner, was a graduate of West Point. His first assignment after school was at Jefferson Barracks in Saint Louis. There he met Julia Dent, whose father was a plantation owner. Although their parents were on opposite sides of the slavery question, Grant and Julia were married after he returned from his assignment in the Mexican War. In the spring of 1852, his garrison was ordered to the Pacific coast. Several of the men were taking their families with them, but Ulysses fortunately discouraged Julia from accompanying him, as she was pregnant with their second child. The garrison sailed from New York to Panama, marched across the Isthmus, and boarded another vessel that took them up the Pacific coast. A cholera epidemic struck when they were crossing Panama, and a third of the men, women, and children died. Grant had promised Julia before he left that as soon as the baby was born and she had regained her strength, he would arrange for them to join him. Now he realized that, unless he acquired a good sum of money on the potato crop, he could not afford to do so. And life at Vancouver was boring. Sometimes only a bottle of whiskey made it bearable.

Oh, Julia, he thought. *If only you were here with me.*

WASHINGTON TERRITORY

It was September before Governor Stevens and his party crossed the summit of the Rockies. When they reached Walla Walla, they learned that the Washington settlers, anxious to bring as many as possible of the 1853 immigrants directly into Puget Sound, had already begun work on a road. When the citizens of Washington learned that McClellan had no immediate plans for road building, they organized a group under Edward J. Allen who were willing to contribute their money, equipment, and time to finish the road.

On October 15, the Columbia newspaper reported, "The Cascade, or Emigrant Road from Walla Walla over the mountains****is finished!"

WASHINGTON, DC

President Pierce advocated the annexation of Hawaii, but his plan fell through when King Kamehameha died.

Hawaii, settled by Polynesians long before Europeans began using the Pacific Ocean as a trading route, had been given the name Sandwich Islands in 1778 by British captain James Cook in honor of the Earl of Sandwich, first Lord of the British Admiralty.

After Cook discovered the islands, whaling ships began stopping there for fresh water and other supplies. The word spread, and by the early 1800s, trading ships were bringing livestock, goods, and plants. New England ships carrying furs to China were putting in at Honolulu for repairs and supplies. In 1820, the American Board of Commissioners for Foreign Missions sent Hiram Bingham and a group of Protestant missionaries to the islands. In 1835 the American firm Ladd and Company opened a sugar plantation. Hawaii had fast become an outpost of New England.

Although Pierce had been unsuccessful in acquiring Hawaii, he had been successful in acquiring more land from Mexico. Upon the advice of Secretary of War Davis, he appointed James Gadsden, a prominent South Carolina railroad man, as minister to Mexico. Gadsden successfully negotiated a $10 million treaty of sale for nearly 30,000 square miles of land that included the region south of the Gila River.

The purchase provided the most advantageous route for a railroad to the Pacific Coast, as the mountains were lower and the track would not have to pass through unorganized territory. Texas was already a state, and New Mexico an organized territory patrolled by federal troops. This fueled rebellion from the northern railroad boosters, who proposed a line running through Nebraska, which was still an unorganized territory.

President Pierce continued to uphold the Compromise of 1850.

EPILOGUE

I n August 1854, a new mail service record was set between Olympia, Washington, and Portland, Oregon. A messenger with Stuart's Express Company covered the 180-mile distance, using steamboat, canoe, and land travel, in thirty-six hours.

President Fillmore sent Commodore Matthew Perry to Japan. With three of Ranald Macdonald's students actively participating in many days of friendly negotiations, an agreement was reached that Americans, on a limited basis, would be welcome in Japan. Ranald continued his travels, visiting many countries before returning to his home in Canada. His family, receiving only the one letter from him, had assumed him dead.

Ulysses Grant's potato venture at Fort Vancouver failed. He resigned from the Army and returned to his family in Missouri.

John McLoughlin, six weeks before his seventy-third birthday, died at his Oregon City home in 1857.

In 1858 the Butterfield Overland Mail Service completed its first trip from Saint Louis to San Francisco in twenty-four days, eighteen hours, and thirty-five minutes.

President Buchanan conferred statehood on Oregon on February 14, 1859. The news was immediately sent over telegraph lines that extended as far as Saint Louis. From there it was rushed to San Francisco by overland stage and on March 15 arrived in Portland by ship. Thirty hours later, the news was in Salem.

Disagreement over the slavery issue between the states continued until Confederate troops attacked Fort Sumter on

April 12, 1861, and the Civil War began. Ulysses Grant returned to military service and became an American hero. The war ended on May 26, 1865, and four years later, Grant was elected president. Indian unrest and disagreements continued in the West until settlement on reservations was established.

In 1862 an Oregon Legislative Act made partial restitution of John McLoughlin's Oregon City land claim to his heirs Eloisa and her second husband, Daniel Harvey. Additional honors were given McLoughlin over the years. In 1907 the Oregon Legislature designated him "Father of Oregon" in recognition of his contribution to the development of Oregon. In 1952 a statue of the doctor was dedicated in Statuary Hall in the Capitol in Washington, DC.

The Union Pacific Railroad was extended west from Omaha and the Central Pacific east from Sacramento. They met in Promontory, Utah, on May 10, 1869.

In 1876 Alexander Graham Bell was perfecting the telephone.

The Transcontinental Canadian Pacific Railroad, running from Montreal to Toronto to Vancouver, was completed in 1885.

Washington gained statehood in 1889. The remainder of the original Oregon Territory was assigned to Montana, Idaho, and Wyoming. Montana gained statehood in 1889; Idaho and Wyoming in 1890.

By 1900 the United States mainland as we know it today was nearly complete: Oklahoma became a state in 1907, and Arizona and New Mexico in 1912.

Alaska was purchased from Russia in 1867 and became the forty-ninth state in 1959. Hawaii became the fiftieth state the same year.

The automobile, so new in the 1890s that it was shown in circuses, became popular. Cross-country highways were built. The radio was developed, followed by experiments with television in the 1920s and 1930s. Airplanes were developed. Charles Lindbergh made the first solo flight across the Atlantic Ocean in 1927. On July 20, 1969, American astronauts visited the moon.

CPSIA information can be obtained at www.ICGtesting.com
Printed in the USA
BVOW04s1549101213

338705BV00002B/9/P